The Capital of Nowhere

Peter Armstrong was born in Blaydon on Tyne in 1957.
He trained as a psychiatric nurse and more recently has worked
as a cognitive therapist in Newcastle. His second collection,
The Red-Funnelled Boat, was published by Picador in 1998.
He lives in Northumberland with his wife and two children.

Peter Armstrong

The Capital of Nowhere

PICADOR

First published 2003 by Picador
an imprint of Pan Macmillan Ltd
Pan Macmillan, 20 New Wharf Road, London N1 9RR
Basingstoke and Oxford
Associated companies throughout the world
www.panmacmillan.com

ISBN 0 330 41267 1

9 8 7 6 5 4 3 2 1

A CIP catalogue record for this book is available from
the British Library.

Typeset by SX Composing DTP, Rayleigh, Essex
Printed and bound in Great Britain by
Mackays of Chatham plc, Chatham, Kent

in memory of Gordon D. Brown

ACKNOWLEDGEMENTS

Poetry Review for 'Steel Guitar Geography',
'Am. Dram. with Weather' and
'Gryke and the Socratic Method'

Salisbury Festival (Last Words) for
'The Dean Surveys the Lingerie Dept'

The Printer's Devil for 'Nehwon'

Contents

Reading Theroux on the 08.24 1

Bellingham 2

Three Sunderland Baptist Songs
    I. The Vision of Jerry Brown 4
    II. The Club Organist at Enon 5
    III. Homage to Joe English 6

Gryke Westrock
    Gryke in Haight-Ashbury 7
    Gryke: the Movie 8
    Gryke and the Socratic Method 9
    Gryke Surveys the Scene of the Siege 10

Between Lord's Shaw and Pit Houses 11

Two Postcards from Mull
    I. A Famous Harbour-View Obscured by Rain 12
    II. God's Civil Engineer 13

Three Laments for the Beautiful Game
    I. Away Leg 14
    II. From the Homeric Programme Notes 15
    III. McIlvanney's Blues 16

Post Mortem for a Princes St Piper 17

Four St Joseph's Wedding Songs
    I. Genius Loci 18
    II. A Heterodox Proper Preface *or* Julian of Eclanum's
        Reply to Augustine 20
    III. End of the Stag Night, Pelaw Station *c.* 1974 21
    IV. A Benediction 22

Steel Guitar Geography 23

Smokescreens 24

Am. Dram. with Weather 26

The Manager as Spiritual Director 27

Nehwon 28

Homo Borealis
I. Sanctuary 30
II. A Hymn to Learning 30
III. Leeks 31
IV. Borealis in Analysis 31
V. Chrysanthemums 32
VI. Spuds 32
VII. Borealis the Hellenist 33

Scranchions
I. Scranchion's History 34
II. Scranchion's Last Stand 35
III. From Scranchion's Laboratory Notebook 35

In Search of the Invisible Poet 36

Charlie Parker on *I Saw the Light* 37

In Memoriam Gordon D. Brown 38

A695 Hymn 40

A Surfboard at Prudhoe Waste Disposal Site 41

Bond *or* The Man with the Golden Bough 42

Dzerzhinski Addresses Joan 43

The Dean Surveys the Lingerie Dept 44

Homage à la Lanterne Rouge 45

The Fall of Byzantium, Stranded West of Blaydon 46

Night Goods 48

Reading Boswell on the 17.11 49

Notes 50

Reading Theroux on the 08.24

I

You keep your place with day returns,
their Out and Back your one lodestone
with every change of altitude
or of regime; the cracked facades
of all those mad,
anoxic, Jesuitical Dorados.

II

At Buenos Morte, then,
the stars come down so close
Cortez had slept in gloves
for fear his hands would burn.
Stranded overnight, you feel
the moon pull at the air you breathe,
the hairs along your forearm rise
less from the cold than gravity.

III

Renounce these drab exotica and return:
the natives will remain oblique;
the wharves along the estuary,
the southernmost basilica
intrinsically out of reach.
Truth and purity
have bedded down with grief.
As the priest said with a laugh:
In a land of the immortals, friend,
the carrion must starve.

Bellingham

Farewell Secret Bellingham,
The capital of Nowhere –
Nowhere, since it never seems
Quite possible to go there.
– Sean O'Brien

Let it stay hidden there like strength . . .
– Philip Larkin

Even Nowhere has its capital,
mispronounced by foreigners
who visit by an accident,
sunlight having camouflaged
the drifting kelp of coal-smoke.

Its histories will be going on,
the grey stone ticking over in the sun,
the four-wheel drives and pick-ups
collecting heat behind the windscreen.
Its grace-notes and its labours blur.

Beyond, there is the forest;
its deep green quilt drawn over
the sleeping figure of the border.
Hidden down its firebreaks
the feral species muster.

But what were you expecting?
Grass is bending double
over the spoil-heaps of the giants,
and imperial roads gone native
lose themselves down farm-tracks.

Here a modest statuary
accommodates the weather,
and the names on stones and shop-fronts
negotiate from era
to different-spoken era.

The bus pulls out; the streetlights
flicker up and spell
You Are Where You Can Get.
The valley settles round that alphabet
hidden there like sense, initiate;

and the wind planes down the reservoir,
the broken wave-heads iridesce;
miles off on the trunk-road
headlights frame a signpost;
they pan across your ceiling and they pass.

Three Sunderland Baptist Songs

(for Ged and Chris Cowburn)

I. THE VISION OF JERRY BROWN

Another midweek meeting
   at some Northern Union satellite
and the Lord of the Air
   has loosed his legions on
   the roof-lead and the vestry window;
serving hatches jammed half-open
   rattle at the backs of fellowships.

But the regenerate Baptist restrooms
   of the saved Midwest!
The gold-plated showerheads!
The prooftexts etched into the mirror so
   you read the Word
   inscribed across your forehead as you rinse!

Consider how suave deacons
   groom themselves before they file onto the stage;
the prairie of a carpet;
the smoked glass foyer that divides
   the badlands from this Eden.

There is a Balm in Gilead, my friends,
a sweet, upholstered elsewhere:
even now approaching
   down these weathered streets of Nineveh,
a limo stretched from Alpha
   to the tail-lights of Omega
   carries us the Marshall Plan of God.
Let's pray.

II. THE CLUB ORGANIST AT ENON

who, rising from a dream of Wurlitzers,
a blessed assembly on sprung maple,
wed Vienna to the City of God
    and we were Marching To Zion in 3/4 time.

O charism of foxtrots!
    the bright black and supple
    mirror of patent leather:
we were waltzing to Zion
    in a sabbath light,
that footloose trinitarian signature
    written by a miracle
    through the white
    sappy heartwood of our limbs,
Now; One two three, One two three, One two three:
    wrapped in a veil of grace-notes
    go Caritas and Eros
One two three, Together two three, Waltz two three;
through the sweet apocryphal circle
    of His judgement.

III. HOMAGE TO JOE ENGLISH

But as to Testimony, I was always an apprentice
to that school of the great extemporizers:
those eloquent and allusive
blue-serge maestros of a style
– dreaming how I'd take the floor
of some late-illumined gallery
and declaim

> *People, I have seen the Doubt:*
the lovely ambiguities of light and dusk.
Who wouldn't wish to share
this cherished jamais vu
of knowing next to nothing?
But now let's pray . . .

> But now let's not:
the sun continuing its slide
on tented crusades and wayside pulpits
is relaxing into unmiraculous charity,
and who'd bear other
than this peaceable dumbstruck witness?

Gryke Westrock

GRYKE IN HAIGHT-ASHBURY

'He came at me with a crowbar: I hit him with Carl Rogers'
– 'Person-Centred Counselling for Undercover Officers',
Northern Californian Police Resource Centre 1979

Halfway through the four-wheel drift
from nth street into nteenth avenue
– the city rolling off the hillside trailing quakes and hoodlums –
having fisted out the bullet-dazzled windscreen
'Straight?' he says, 'How come?'

The white-faced sidekick
glues himself in the passenger seat;
Control scrapes on beneath *Live Dead*
and his own imagined *Requiem for Jerry*
dreaming its great spirals through his head.

Later, in the half-lit target range
he shuts his eyes and aims
at the concentric rings of white:
tantric master of his 45,
exhaling with each clean, invisible hit.

GRYKE: THE MOVIE

I. End Frame

The squad cars are arriving now;
the bodies have arranged themselves.
You turn your back on everything
and let the badge or documents
drop. And now the camera pans
across the street and now the town
and now the sky. Music plays.

II. After the Credits

You'll still be walking when we've left this place,
a low-built town behind you and the scrublands stretched
    ahead;
phone-lines looping into nowhere, footprints half submerged
    in sand.
You check your print against the one, and then the next . . .

GRYKE AND THE SOCRATIC METHOD

The tape whirs, or the striplight; or
the breathing of a guard becomes
everything that isn't some
tie between inquisitor

and the one who longs to tell.
(*Telling now would be a joy.*)
Everything is miles away:
this room, a siren somewhere, all

that falls outside the circle of
your face, your arms, my arms, my face.
How long need we go on with this?
(*How much have you the need to prove?*)

The tape whirs, or the day outside
creeps up the avenues and revs
the engines on a million drives.
Beyond the city limits ride

our visions of the interstates:
perspective-exercising roads
whose lonely fugitives are gods
that nobody interrogates.

GRYKE SURVEYS THE SCENE OF THE SIEGE

Gryke Surveys the Scene of the Siege
You read diamonds in the shattered pane:
every whispered hymn to tact,
all negotiation come to kristallnacht,
that fractured edge, this stain.

For all that, this beauty:
the squad cars' lights, like genii,
stoppered in a million shards, that I
must sift until a done duty

gifts me the wounds of Padre Pio.
Or look at the way that glass
has found a home beneath the skin, as
you, and I, and these of the brief cameo

have found our comfort deep within
each others' versions of events,
so, once the friendly fire relents,
you read diamonds in the shattered pane.

Between Lord's Shaw and Pit Houses

(Sheet 80 NY821926)

At the back end of beyond
the only signpost musters
a rimless wheel of arrows
pointing everywhere.
You let the engine idle
– the wind exhaling
through an open slit of window,
a ditch of rushes
bowing to the inevitable –
and could almost reach and pluck
from that faintly ringing metal
it beckons not; it beckons
each place-name like a petal
till the obvious is clear
where was it you were going?
It must be somewhere here.

Two Postcards from Mull

I. A FAMOUS HARBOUR-VIEW OBSCURED BY RAIN

It's Sabbath
and there's nine tenths of the great blue bruise of Celtdom shut.
We're holed up at the pier-head cafe,
waiting for the rain to clear, the lonely hour of commerce
to discomfit presbyteries across the island.
Now try to tease the sky out from the sea:
close your eyes and conjure
that clear dividing firmament. Or give it up for lost,
like so much mainland, another legion
disappeared up some or other glen. Remember,
this was never weather: this stuff
is theology.

II. GOD'S CIVIL ENGINEER

From the triple-decker pulpit at Loch Grief
you look clear through Telford's windows
to the rooftops of Geneva.
O, the Powers and Dominions!
Ecclesia LMS beneath
the pure unblinking study
of a transcendent Fat Controller;
whose permanent way being narrow,
what place for the frills of masons
where rigour speaks to rigour?
Now crockets, buffets, cupolas
dissolve before the Other;
across a railless island
the cloud smears into heather.

Three Laments for the Beautiful Game

I. AWAY LEG

It's somewhere you'd take days to reach:
the towns, the stadia that bleach
beneath those skies and politics.

The crowd has come in from the sticks
and stunted decades that obtain
beyond sports pages and the rain

to stand at epic distances
where, knowing their attendance is
as much a duty as a right,

they nail their anthems to the pulse.
The floodlights plant the seeds of night.
This always will be somewhere else.

II. FROM THE HOMERIC PROGRAMME NOTES

Picture how the wind, when it comes down off the moors
and drives across some dale or plain,
sets the barley moving in long hushing waves
rehearsing that great anthem it will sing
when, dolphin-leaping one last spit of sand,
it goes its way to sea: just so, the end behind the goal
poured people down the terracing in waves
the instant that the keeper, grasping nothing,
came to ground and bit the trodden earth
and threadbare grass of the six-yard box . . .

III. McILVANNEY'S BLUES

Snow is blowing down the Munich runway;
across the whole of Lanarkshire
the winding gear slops over
in among with so much scrim.

A generation marching out in monochrome
– parallel elevens with a rain
that burns between their stoic faces
and the screen –

must be talking other dialects.
You can lip-read their outlying districts:
the close, benighted villages where

the radio match comes over now;
the foreign field, the cold flight back;
the sky that true unvisionable black

Post Mortem for a Princes St Piper

I

He turns up in the Water of Leith,
limbs adrift in a waterlogged saltire,
his wafting Black Watch
showing everything.

II

Observe the skin's north-facing pallor;
the finger-pads red-ringed
from years of pibroch
under Scott's long shadow.

III

Stand him trebles in his stripped-down bar.
Stand second in his stairwell duel.
Hand him to his startled double
rushing up to meet him from below.

Four St Joseph's Wedding Songs

(for Sarah Armstrong and Alistair Stokoe)

I. GENIUS LOCI

'I've observed that when certain phases of the moon fall into
sequence with certain details of the liturgical calendar, you
can hear – very faintly, mind: you have to know what you'd be
listening for – that legendary catarrh of Fr. O'Donaghue, or
some remembrance of those Rosaries he used say in that kind
of Galway Sanskrit of his'

   – *McGurk's Mythologies*, 2nd edn, Knights of St Columba Publications

Just reconstruct
   those cruel hours in the sea:
   the alveoli slicked with swallowed crude
so he could hardly summon
   Star of the Ocean
let alone his breath
   (and so ever after);

and who'd grudge him the night off
   thin-aired Purgatory's slopes?
Listen and you'll hear him rummaging
   for that blend he'd spent
   those years of early hours perfecting,
chasing that one
   phlegm-incising draught,
measuring his peak flow
   against the glow of a gobbet of charcoal.

So consider yourselves amphibian:
that generation first to nose
    its way onto the tidal mud,
the immensities of light
    that must have felt like drowning.

II. A HETERODOX PROPER PREFACE
or JULIAN OF ECLANUM'S REPLY TO AUGUSTINE

Now let your bed be aired
   in some civil Pelagian loggia,
love being forever in cahoots
with the decent
   conscience of heresy,

while St Orthodoxus,
   with his shame at the body's
lovely absurdities,
we'll commend to the benevolent
   analysis of heaven,
the sly restitution
   of his dumped old mistress

III. END OF THE STAG NIGHT, PELAW STATION. *c.* 1974

(for Keith Newton and Tim Hughs)

His head lolled back like a gored toreador's, or a boxer's killed in the ring. The gate of Troy unbreached another day, they laid him on the slatted bench graffitoed with his eulogies, and left him to our ministrations while they zig-zagged off to fetch a cab.

A coal train should have run through lamenting deeply; the coke works should have set the cloud pulsing red and black. We should have faced that way and sang The Wedding March (the Hendrix version, Stornaway Festival, 1967)

IV. A BENEDICTION

Now let your bed be cut adrift
    that for the night you lose yourselves
and every hint of harbour-light
    far out in that shoreless gulf

which, when you've trekked so far inland
    the cloud remits and rivers halt,
will come in the gull-shouts of a squall,
    an unpetitioned edge of salt.

Steel Guitar Geography

I

Since it's proven *We're All Lonely*,
all confessees at that same roadside bar,
all biblically athirst
in the dry places of the heart,

make mine a bitter;
lead me from the jukebox weeping;
wed me to the Queen of Nowhere
whose sorrow is for keeps

II

And here's Safety, Nebraska, population us,
its houses wagon-ringed against the night,
a wheatscape dark enough
to show these window-lights from space.

Now should the moon ignite
the gravel at the side of the road,
surely this is where we longed to be:
not less lonely, but perfected in it

III

After line dancing at the Masonic
cats' eyes half the darkness;
the telephone wires' deep harmonic
plays it how it is

Smokescreens

(for Ivy Blackburn)

Shouldn't it have been
Hume, diagnosing the facts
    through a dreich Auld Reekie smore
    before
Kant, serene
    beneath Germanic skies
who saw
the milky skin
    of cataract
    between
the seer and the seen?

Hence this fug
    of thought and nicotine:
the dialectic
    fag-smoke's
    playing out with light,
carving queries in a slant of sun
    we otherwise
    would never have seen.

Ivy,
    ask another one:
fix us with that sceptic's
    cool, appraising eye
and freeze the frame
    before it's run
with *So:*
    let's you and I

consider just exactly how
you know you know;

since, now the haar
    drifts up from Leith,
the fret
    from one or other Shields,
either we must muddle with
    or learn to love
    the grey it builds:
that cloud of partial knowing whose
    is dissolves into its *seems*,
and leaves us here to navigate
this smoke that might (or not)
    hide flames.

Am. Dram. with Weather

(for the Wylam Amateur Dramatic Society)

It's Friday night at the Institutes:
along the valley-side the rain
is rubbing out the land with its
cold attentions and its grey

swab across the villages,
lines you've got half by the heart
tapping on the window ledge
from inside, like the rain from out.

Now everyone is close to pals;
has been and will be here again:
the thumb-prints in the pitch-pine walls
matched exactly to the grain

so if you dry, or if you corpse,
the empty rooms will read you in
where silence is the art of lapse,
and, coming back years on, you yearn

for somewhere that this might have been,
or was, or will be (you'll forget);
but now the props, the boards, the rain,
the no-man's-land behind the set,

decline to comment on the text
(the best is silence anyway);
an old retainer genuflects;
outsiders look, and look away.

The Manager as Spiritual Director

(Neil Andrew: Southend to Doncaster Rovers, £10,000, March 2000)

Go, son,
    to that Santiago de Compostela
      of the scar-tissued and clapped-out

where silence
    celebrating every goal
      will discipline the heart,

the dark night of the soul,
    my son,
      being at the northern edge of sight.

Embrace its blessed negatives:
    the absoluteness of its lack
      of hoardings, people, terraces and lights.

The watching absence at your back
    sets up another wordless chant:
      it is your soul that echoes it.

Nehwon

If it were the case that you had woken
stranded where the trains had given over
waiting in the rain beside the river,
platforms gone to blackberry and bracken;

crossing by the bridge above the weir
(strung between an always and the never)
surely you would find beyond the river
villages of Institute and spire

where, for all the labours of the weather
chiselling exactly and forever
sliver after sliver after sliver,
time had bound its aggregates together.

Dialects that come to the air untroubled
clear above the quarrels of the weir
mark you as the only stranger here
instantly, and place you with the fabled

denizens of any other era.
Everything is running to its schema:
manners, newsprint, adverts, roadsigns, grammar;
all that keeps its word to pay the bearer

where the myth that nothing lasts forever
bows before the civil weight of detail.
Had you been found shivering and foetal
washed up with the wrack beside the river,

how long you had slept is not the matter
nor that you are aged or an infant:
strangers take your hand and for a moment
bid you to attend to how the water

trundles by with neither past nor future;
visit in their gaze a kind of pity
(were you, in the end, to choose the city:
bright, inconstant, altogether other)

Homo Borealis

(for Anne Garland)

I. Sanctuary

You find him hunkered in his shed,
his offerings to Demeter
    placed, just so, around him
    in his corn-king's bower:
leeks, chrysanthemums, spuds.

II. A Hymn to Learning

He looks up to his northern sky
and names the constellations:
The Running Dog,
Thin Seam, The Hewer.

All his classes are night:
Dark Matter
for his thorough mind
to worry at

knowing that
the biggest stars
are still coal-black
and waiting to take.

III. Leeks

All flesh being grass,
again he must dig over
the one unfathomable trench.

How else to read
such tender mercies
and the weight behind the blade?

Adam's *marra familia*
indiscriminately hinnying
Jehovah, Eve, The Lads.

IV. Borealis in Analysis

And then their yearning for the Mothergate,
squirming in from it as far as they can get,
obstetricians of the seam;
as if they couldn't pick
their wish out from their dread
their death- out from their marriage-bed
(though dark warm walls engulf their every dream).

Listen to them:
Mamma, Marra; Marra, Maam:
as if they couldn't tell each other,
being so extremely black,
apart from one another
or their precious Mothergate,
or whether, having once gone in,
they should ever find the black road back

V. Chrysanthemums

Watch him while he preens each globe
as if it were a woman's hair
and he St Paul, to know the meaning
of such glory.

VI. Spuds

When he lifts a clinch of roots
the earth coming off their skins
is holy Russia's:

her host of ill uses;
her black bread crumbs
her (darkling) love.

When he turns his face up-over
his eyes catch whole
the sky from High Spen round to Marley Hill

and distil
a Baltic in the iris
and weep amber

VII. Borealis the Hellenist

Of late, he steps into the river twice
and finds the same river;

seeking to explain, has stumbled
to his full Socratic doubt.

Between The Club and the Gymnasium;
between The Lads and the Death of Labour

has learned whisper
Aah knaa nowt, me.

Ask him anything;
tease him till he spits

Aah divvent knaa

Scranchions

(for Dale Huey)

Scranchion *n.*   A mutterer, one not likely to be believed (from M. English *Scrantion*, a scrap of batter or other food, too small to be served alone)

– Wrekenton's Dictionary of Fraud and Fable

I. Scranchion's History

Scranchion heaves his face towards the sun
from the glint of clay in the furrow,
the smoke of fog in the cup of the land.
Bugger it mutters Scranchion,
the bolus of his hockle rolling on his tongue,
Bugger, Pissing Bastard, Fuck.

All his weight comes up into his gob,
all his glottals blunder to a stop.

Bugger. Hockle.
Bugger. Howk.

II. Scranchion's Last Stand

He plugs his wounds and scans the field:
the 27th destroyed; the colours down;
the Mad Nawab, his golden tooth still glinting in the sun,
brandishing his stolen Wisdens,
cobbling a throne of Hansards,
gold-bound first editions of *The Soldier's Scott.*

Dammit all, sir mutters Scranchion
(the sabres are tintinnabulating in his ear)
Dammit, sir! aloud
(the playingfields; the House;
the generations swimming off forever,
clean as Captain Webb)

III. From Scranchion's Laboratory Notebook

Instead the rats composed themselves
    into the face of Skinner,
Padesky's wheel of thought,
the gothic spires and oriels
    of that latest dream of GAD.

All our sweet hypotheses
    nulled amongst those finials.
Our half-completed papers
    dancing where we set them on the wind,

we took our vows of silence
    and went east.

In Search of the Invisible Poet

Try to pick him out
against the timber-yards, the cool, intestinal refineries,
his myth of the Pit.

Speak his name aloud in any bar,
as if to merely summon him,
would bring him out of purdah,

as if his people, humourless and avid,
wouldn't to a man announce
I'm Spartacus, eyes void

or fixed on all that history,
the parochial depths he's promised them.
But there he goes, shy and beery

through the back yard into elegy,
hugging to himself
the cleared streets, the edgy

acrid breeze that stands
for everything he still declines to tell:
the means and ends

he shrinks from as a kind of duty;
the strategies he disavows
from conscience, or from art, or else from pity.

Charlie Parker on *I Saw The Light*

Beyond the Kansas city limits,
darkness yearns
– our only true supplier, Hank,
our one true audience

In Memoriam Gordon D. Brown

So now let all the hawthorns
    down every line and waggonway
from Warden Law
    to the ghost of Elvet station

shed their off-white blossom
    and that honeyed, soured fragrance
as if hearing that your civil
    socialist voice had quietened.

Versed, knowing, liberal,
    you improvised a harmony
from the tunes of Pound and Bevan,
    stiff Reith and wild red Guthrie.

Now, if there were a heaven,
    the Troubadours would be tuning
their sweet arcane instruments
    to meet you off the ferry;

the sunlight on the river
    (be it Rhône or be it Wear)
would light you to the scriptorium
    or the love-feasts of Le Baux.

But tonight the stream flows sadly
    without gleam or erudition
as if the inanimate
    had felt your hurt

and if I saw you walking
    towards Dragonville to meet us,
when the weary early evening
    throws up dust in ghosts behind us,

you would tell me how delusion
    offers to the grieving
the honeyed scent of hawthorn
    and denies the thorn.

You chose, like your father,
    another, unlit exit.
The dumb sun rising
    from its coal-dredging ocean

had it the wit, would darken
    knowing you were gone.

A695 Hymn

(for William Martin)

Meanwhile I'm shifting up to fifth along
this road across the landfill
past all those lyric fictions
villages have taken for a name:
Star Gate, Greenside, Clara Vale
– a glance of street-lights
and a figure in the kitchenette.

The city shrinking in the mirrors,
its strings of neon threading black,
dreams this valley and its southerlies,
this fine rain glazing terrace roofs,
this silhouette the one lit window catches.

A Surfboard at Prudhoe
Waste Disposal Site

He has forsaken California:
the in-turning curl of the wave,
its lucent tunnel wrapping him around with green,
he relinquishes
to be as Buddha to the grey-faced town;

where now he minds
the rooftop spume of smoke;
or, now, the mote-flecked air
between his eye and the light-soaked
window of the bar;

or, now he rocks his child to sleep
and the groundswell takes him in its arms,
goes cradled and unclinging
where her slight pacific breathing
is the current of his dreams

and he can ride
the Whin Sill scarp face
infinitely slowly north,
the ages coming one by one adrift
like foam beneath his feet.

Bond
or The Man with the Golden Bough

Sex and death have proven one.
What Mt Carmel's climbers won
by such slow denial then,
simplifies beneath this sun
that equally lights breast and gun;
the spring queen and the king of corn

tied together dancing, so
where he goes, there she must go,
circling the bed both know
stands there both before and for
the oubliette awaiting, O!
so sad and aptly for her; though

they couple without hope or love
as if the discipline might prove
how abnegation should contrive
joys for those who rise above
the merely tender. See, they waive
their right to trial (and she, to live).

But cut from Monaco to ice
where let the tundra teach us grace,
as Thanatos comes darkling face
to face with lust, and owns he knows
those features in the screen's dark glass
which now (of course) he lifts to us.

Dzerzhinski Addresses Joan

Inside me an East European Poet is trying to get out
– Joan Hewitt

You do not know these flats, woman:
the stew of cabbage simmering
    on every landing's common primus;
the true collective grief
    that only we
        could raise to verse.

Gatesheadgorod in a wet month:
bedraggled fans Transponder Rostov
    brought to decorate the rain
are sheltering against The Manager's Tomb.
Inverted workers, welded to our soles
    each morning as we tread the cobbled mirror
        of the People's Square
are bleeding with remembrances
    of Ladas and Trabants,
        of lead-weight cameras,
the mass editions of MacDiarmid
    printed to withstand the Bomb.

But tell your Windsors
    and the Beckhams we remain,
our children learning other languages,
our fathers failing to acknowledge us
    as, half asleep, we greet them in the glass,
and fingering our rusting
    standard-issue razors murmur:
        Comrades, everything must pass.

The Dean Surveys the Lingerie Dept

Fifth column
    in a theocracy of woollens!
Consider how the nave might entertain
    these metaphysical underwirings;
    the conceits of silk;
how the black spines of Prayer Books
    might nustle up this close against
an unreformed incense
    of satins and the skin.

O! Decorated of the flesh!
    Chartres of the curvatures!
Fan vault singing praises of the breast!
How many lenten disciplines
    might we come to love,
how many pure transcendent chills
if they teased us to epiphany?
    – immanences, immanences;
trappings of the rite . . .

Homage à la Lanterne Rouge

Between the Col of the Dead Man Walking
and the Col de la Couronne d'Épines,
he has dredged this hallucinosis
from the silt of dead endorphins,

the people having turned to leeches,
the road to glass, and then to sand;
his heartbeat, when it steadies to a signature,
being given to the drummer of his funeral band.

Even this year's slogans, slithering the asphalt,
have begun to tell a story
– how of a night
when old men had seen off their eau-de-vie

and staggered up the coffin-road towards the ridge,
there passed them on that *via dolorosa*
breathing hard but silently
a martyr in the final throes.

They give him just one push towards the top,
one valedictory *Allez!*
before they recollect the face
and that the road goes nowhere now –

as this one does,
which has become the route-map of his veins;
his heart that Paris where the Arc de Triomphe, wrapped in black,
looks down upon a crowd stood silent and immense.

The Fall of Byzantium,
Stranded West of Blaydon

(for Arriva Trains)

I summon here the guardians of decline:
the sad Comneni, the half-wit house of Angelus,
the great and hopeless Paleologi
who, fitterless, must occupy
a singing throne gone dumb
(Apostles' equals, scavenging for scraps)

as we, all sweat and outbreathed air
must wait another hour and watch
the vacant track-beds settle,
the foxgloves edge towards us,
till train, till track, till town, till age
are given to the river or the moss.

Drivers and conductors
dispute the *filioque*
– *regulator* in the Latin wanting
certain finer points of Greek –
and we pray for a man with a spanner,
approaching (please God) as we speak

from Carlisle or from Venice
and their gold-rich saving West.
But hour succumbs to hour, and soon
the sky will surely lighten
on the last day of an empire
and the cut of the sickle moon.

The bindweed and the willowherb
will have scrawled across the Land Walls
or the line been axed beneath us;
bugle, buttercup, bitter vetch
have twined around your heel
and pulled.

That the janissaries of green
might wash to the essential
this that cannot now recover
– icon, railhead, porphyry;
the gleaming arcane mechanisms
that imaged a Prime Mover –

disembark, citizens.
Descend these embankments
of cinders and bracken
to where the walls stand open
on a different country
and the skylarks rising.

Night Goods

Now the roads forget themselves
in Linear B, redundant morse,
the peaceful sequences of lights.

But in their high, lit vantages
the signalmen are gods
who throw the lever on the night
and watch it track from stretch to stretch

till, our of sight and into thought,
you feel its rumble underfoot,
the tremor when you touch the pane

Reading Boswell on the 17.11

(after Michael Longley)

Now let Stranraer stand for Ultima Thule,
or, changing at some rain-hit Gallowegian halt,
pitch yourself amongst those fogs and dialects,
their uncouth sprawl of firths and mulls,
that fabulous extreme, the Hebrides.

That the monumental brain might yet
browbeat the elements into submission,
parse each vestige of a dead tongue
found visiting the living,
each mute subordinate shadow
of a former dispensation;

that the dead – *were it permitted* –
might come back to us,
their definitions all at sea,
dispensing all the favours they withheld,
easing from its mind's brilliant grip
that sad, dystonic body.

Notes

Bellingham
'Ingham' endings in Northumberland place names are predominantly pronounced 'ingjum'. Larkin's 'Show Saturday' was written after a visit to the annual agricultural show at Bellingham.

Three Sunderland Baptist Songs
The Northern Union is a kind of Baptist diocese.

Gryke Westrock
The title is a very bad, inverted sort of pun. Limestone pavements have two kinds of split in the stone, one lateral, the other vertical. One is a clint and the other is a grike.

Carl Rogers: father of non-directive, or person-centred counselling.

Jerry: Jerry Garcia, of the Grateful Dead.

Two Postcards From Mull
LMS: London, Midland and Scottish Railway.

A Heterodox Proper Preface
Julian of Eclanum took heretical issue with St Augustine of Hippo's view that any pleasure in the sexual act was inherently sinful.

Smokescreens
Prof. I. M. Blackburn has been a key figure in establishing Cognitive Therapy as a mainstream treatment for depression on this side of the Atlantic. Whether in Edinburgh or Newcastle, she conducted a one-woman rearguard action against NHS no-smoking policies.

Homo Borealis

The Mothergate is the main road into or through a coal mine.
Marra: mate, friend.

Scranchions

Dr Huey dubiously asserts that 'scranchion' is a Gateshead term
for the little bits of batter that come with chips.
GAD: Generalized Anxiety Disorder.

Bond

Mt Carmel: See *The Ascent of Mt Carmel*, St John of the Cross.

A695 Hymn

See William Martin's 'A19 Hymn', in *Cracknrigg* (Taxus, 1983).

Homage à la Lanterne Rouge

The Lanterne Rouge is the rider ranked last overall in the Tour de
France.

The Fall of Byzantium

Angelus has a hard 'g'. The *Filioque* is that passage in the creed
which divides Eastern and Western churches. The issue is whether
the Holy Spirit proceeds from the Father *and* the Son (the Western
view) or from the Father alone (the Eastern view). *Jannisaries*
were the crack troops of the Ottomans. A sickle moon was in the
sky on the morning of the fall of Byzantium.

Reading Boswell

See Michael Longley's 'Dr Johnson on the Hebrides' and 'Dr
Johnson Dying', in *No Continuing City* (Macmillan, 1969).

ISSAC Y.

The Midnight Express And Other Short Stories

Contents

Preface   iv

The Midnight Express   1

The Post-It Puzzle   20

The Plight Of The Nicholas   32

  CHAPTER I   32

    CHAPTER II   39

    CHAPTER III   43

    CHAPTER IV   48

    CHAPTER V   53

    EPILOGUE   57

The Robbery   58

  STANLEY   58

  TOMMY   59

  TED   66

  MARY   73

  GEORGE   74

Preface

This book is a collection of 4 short stories I wrote that I thought would be better to publish into one collective book than to publish them individually on a platform. The first story I wrote was actually *The Plight Of The Nicholas* during the summer of 2022. During the late summer period, I was inspired by this YouTube Short: https://www.youtube.com/watch?v=n4Apwq kxeHg to write the *Post-It Puzzle*, and fun fact, my favorite out of all these stories is actually the *Post-It Puzzle*. I consider it my finest work in this book. I wrote *The Midnight Express* next, during Christmastime all the way into February, and it is quite obvious I drew inspiration there from Chris Van Allsburg's *The Polar Express*, although both stories are wildly different. (you'll see) Originally, This book was just going to be 3 stories, but at the last minute I had a brilliant idea I knew couldn't go to waste, so I worked as fast as I could and finished *The Robbery* in just a few days. I didn't know I can write that fast. After proofreading and correcting the countless mistakes I made and formatting the book, I then designed the cover, which the train in the cover art was generated by DALL-E 2: https://openai.com/product/da ll-e-2.

Thank you in advance for picking up this book and reading it, I hope you do enjoy this quick read. If you do end up enjoying it, please leave a review. If don't end up enjoying it, leave a review as well explaining why you didn't exactly enjoy it, it will help me improve in the future.

The Midnight Express

* * *

J onathan Banks was dead, to begin with. That is certain. At the age of 22, Banks was diagnosed with stage 1 cancer, and at the age of 24, Banks was diagnosed with stage 4 cancer. He passed away a few months later on the 4th day of April. Dr. Fernandez submitted the report hours after, after which his body was moved to the morgue. Twenty days later, a 30-minute funeral service was held for Banks at Chapelworth Cemetery, where his family and loved ones mourned his loss. His coffin was lowered into the grave and buried, and a gravestone was placed.

At the stroke of midnight, Banks awakened from his slumber. Surrounded by a cemetery, he found himself standing atop his own grave, as if by some otherworldly force. Strangely, he appeared to be a mere apparition - his body was translucent and exuded a subtle, yet distinct greenish hue. His feet were not in direct contact with the ground and instead hovered slightly above the coarse, brown earth. Banks donned a simple ensemble comprising a shirt, jacket, trousers, and sneakers, coupled with his favorite sports cap.

After several moments of disorientation, Banks came to the daunting realization that he had passed away, his final moments of life and the tearful farewell of his father flooding back to him. With this revelation, Banks knew that he had been transformed into a ghost, a phantom, a spirit that roamed the earth. Above him, the crescent moon radiated a splendid light, casting a soft, ethereal glow over the cemetery.

Suddenly, Banks was jarred by a high-pitched, piercing sound, resembling a shrill whistle that echoed throughout the grave-yard. Instinctively, he looked around, trying to pinpoint the source of the sonorous noise, only to hear a loud and repetitive thumping sound. Gradually, the noise grew louder and closer, sounding more like a train's chugging locomotive. An enormous steam 4-6-2 express train, shimmering in a greenish glow, materialized out of nowhere and hurtled towards Banks. The train consisted of several passenger coaches, all transparent and ghostly, causing Banks to suspect that this apparition was a phantom train. With its whistle sounding loudly, the locomotive rolled towards Banks before grinding to a halt. Miraculously, rails appeared under the train as it approached.

The train was a majestic, yet ancient, locomotive, radiating a bright glow in the darkness. It had a gleaming black livery was adorned with two short side-plates on either side of the front, while steam and smoke emanated from its chimney. Its small headlamp, situated atop the chimney, emitted a modest beam of light, and its nameplate, etched in what appeared to be silver, read 'The Midnight Express.'

Suddenly, the front coach's door swung open, and a ghost, dressed in a black conductor's uniform, emerged from it.

"So, this is Chapelworth Cemetery, and you are a fresh burial, by the name of..." the conductor produced a clipboard, and continued. "Jonathan Banks."

Banks was stunned and rendered speechless by the sight of a phantom express train materializing right before him and did not produce a reply.

"Hello? Am I speaking to the ghost of Jonathan Weatherby Banks?" the conductor inquired, waving his hand in front of Banks' face.

"Y-yes," Banks replied. "Um, what- how- what-"

"To answer your confusion, Mr. Banks, this is the Midnight Express. At midnight, we transport recently deceased souls to the underworld, where you will face judgment to proceed to the afterlife, or if you're unlucky, to burn eternally in the fires of hell."

Still in shock and reeling from this surreal encounter, Banks nodded his head weakly, and the conductor led him inside the coach, but then Banks froze in his tracks.

"What's the matter?" the conductor asked impatiently. "Time's a-wastin'!"

"Um-" Banks struggled with his words as he looked back on the world around him. The shining moon casting a soft light on the landscape. The cemetery, the trees swaying in the wind. In the distance, he could hear the roar of an actual train passing by. Sounds of late-night commuters, in their cars and the hum of their engines. The soft song of nightingales, and the cries of crows. The world he will leave behind. "Can I- not go?"

"What are you talking about?" The conductor asked, his tone restless.

"I've lived for so- little, seen so little things," Banks said. "Can I remain in the living world, as a ghost? I want to- I mean, don't ghosts-"

"Of course not!" The conductor said sharply. "The idea is ridiculous. We are on a tight schedule, and we must not dilly-dally! You are due for the underworld! Come on!" Without further warning, he clutched Banks by his shirt collar, pushed him onto the carriage, shut the door behind him, and blew his whistle.

The coach's interior was dimly lit by several spaced-out lanterns, casting a soft glow over the rows of leather seats housing other ghosts. The large and dirty windows obscured the surroundings somewhat.

Banks sat down in one of the seats and tried making himself comfortable. With the shrill noise of the steam whistle chiming, the train started crawling forwards, accelerating slowly. Exhaust steam and smoke puffed out of the chimney, increasing in rate as the train increased in speed until a continuous stream of exhaust shot out of it. Out the carriage window, Banks could see the surrounding landscape, illuminated by the moonlight, as the train passed. They crawled slowly out of the cemetery and onto a road, where his theory of a phantom express was confirmed by the fact that the train passed through an entire house without any struggle, among other solids. A row of shops, a lamppost, and a school. His hometown went by, the familiar houses, the church, the streetlamps, shops, and schools, until eventually they passed by even his own house. A brick-built formation that was part of a large development around the area. Memories and nostalgia flooded Bank's dead brain and his entire body, sending shivers into his veins. The arguments his father had with the neighbors about ridiculous topics such as soccer and the soap opera. His birthdays, his school life, then his first job at the local fast food restaurant, then the second in his uncle's law firm after he'd finished his higher education. Well, of course, it went downhill from there with his sickness. If ghosts could cry, Banks would've teared up ages ago. He didn't want to go. Despite having all sorts of treatments, the stupid disease managed to claim his life. Now he was on this ghost train to- what did the conductor say? The underworld? He didn't see why he couldn't simply stay in the living world as a ghost and observe those around him.

As the train accelerated, its speed increased at an alarming rate, causing the express to hurtle forward with a deafening roar. The rhythmic chugging of the wheels echoed through the coach's walls, drowning out all other sounds. Fogs of exhaust belched out of the chimney, adding to the sensation of acceleration.

Banks held on tightly to the handrails, feeling his heart rate, although he was dead, somehow quicken with each passing moment. The train continued to gain momentum, exceeding the limits of a typical steam locomotive by more than just a margin. As he gazed out of the window, the surroundings became a blur, passing by in a mere blink of an eye.

The moonlit landscape that once stretched out before him soon dissolved into nothingness, swallowed up by the void that surrounded them. The train hurtled forward at an unimaginable speed, accelerating with no end in sight. The vast expanse of nothingness seemed to stretch out endlessly, a daunting and endless abyss that made the passengers feel as if they were hurtling into oblivion.

The train then in the span of a blink, very slowly, started decelerating. When the express stopped, Banks could see they were in a completely different setting. It was a completely different cemetery. It seemed there was another soul to pick up. Afterward, the train started up again and they were on their way.

As the express train continued to hurtle forward, its velocity only seemed to increase, with the wheels clattering loudly against the iron rails, creating a roar that almost drowned out the sonorous chugging of the locomotive. The landscape outside became a mere blur, as they hurtled deeper into the darkness, faster than ever before. The exhaust from the chimney was now billowing out in great storms, spewing forth with such force that even those in the back brake-van could hear it. The train itself began to lurch wildly from side to side, causing the passengers to grip the handrails with an iron grip, their spectral fingers turning a ghastly shade of white. It was like a theme-park ride, or being on a ship amid a raging storm. Banks could feel the entire train bouncing up and down uncontrollably, and he feared at any moment, they would fly off the rails and plummet into oblivion.

The ear-splitting clanging and chugging of the wheels only added to the terror of the moment, and Banks imagined that the axles would dislocate and fly off, or the wheels would launch out of place like a cannonball, or even the safety valve of the train would burst uncontrollably. The coaches themselves were now clanging loudly, their wheels simply not designed for such speed. They scraped, creaked, and cracked as the sparks flew off violently from the rails. It was a wonder that they hadn't derailed yet, or that the entire train hadn't simply disintegrated into pieces.

But then, an even more ear-piercing whistle of the train over-came all the other clanging and cracking as Banks felt they finally started to slow down, even for just a fraction. They plunged slowly out of the endless void and into what appeared to be a dark cave, deep underground. The wheels stopped clanging as loudly and by a miracle stayed in place, and so did the axles.

As they meandered through the obsidian tunnel, the rhythmic chugging of the locomotive was almost calming, like a lullaby in the stillness of the night. But suddenly, the peace was shattered by a blinding flash of orange light up ahead. Somehow, the train was now passing through a waterfall of searing lava. The heat that emanated from the source was so intense that it seared Banks' skin, causing him to recoil in agony. The suffocating atmosphere was enough to cause discomfort even to the departed souls.

As they emerged from the molten lava, miraculously unscathed, they resumed their journey through the somber cave. Ahead of them, a dilapidated structure, resembling a station, gradually came into view. The decrepit edifice was coated in a thick layer of dust and looked as though it had weathered the ravages of time. The platform, riddled with an intricate web of cracks, appeared as if it could crumble to dust at any moment. The dimly lit lanterns of the station, casting a feeble glow, were the only light source that could be discerned amidst the gloom.

The express came to a gradual and precise halt at the station, as if a moment of serenity had befallen the train. The piercing sound of the locomotive's whistle echoed throughout the platform, indicating that their journey had come to an end. The steam escaping from the locomotive's cylinder produced a hissing noise akin to a sigh of relief.

The conductor's voice resounded throughout the station, perhaps through a concealed speaker, though the quality of the sound indicated that the equipment was old and worn. "Welcome to the entrance of the underworld," he announced. "Here, you will be subjected to a trial, the results of which will determine if you are worthy to enter the afterlife. Failure to pass any of these trials will result in eternal suffering in the fires of hell. Once you enter the afterlife, you will remain there for a minimum of one lifetime before you are allowed to reincarnate into the surface world. During your stay in the afterlife, you will be permitted to visit the surface world at ordained times. Now, please disembark."

The coach doors automatically swung open, and the souls began to exit the train. Banks, however, remained at the rear of the coach, seemingly held back by something. Shock, perhaps. Bewilderment. To be candid, who wouldn't be? Death is certainly a *unique* experience. He was now in the underworld, a place that he never postulated to exist. When he disembarks he would go to trial, a trial for his life. Nevertheless, he eventually made his way to the platform. As he watched the train depart, he couldn't help but feel relieved. The ride had been far too rough and chaotic for his liking.

A throng of souls congregated at the platform, their collective presence swelling as they streamed into a narrow doorway, and then into an even more confined hallway. As Banks emerged from the passageway, he found himself in a magnificent grand hall. The hall was a study in darkness, with black, grey, and somber hues accented by blue lanterns and fiery blue flames. The bright-crimson carpet underfoot provided a striking contrast to the surrounding shadows. At the far end of the hall, Banks could discern a grand throne made of obsidian, atop which sat a figure that looked like a man, but was nothing of the sort. This being had pallid, ghastly-gray skin, draped in flowing, raven-black robes that framed crow-like wings. A crown of thorns adorned its head, and its visage was one of wrath and intimidation, exuding an aura of terror that could be felt both within and without. Flanking the throne in a line of tiered stands were ghosts, outfitted in what appeared to be formal robes. There were even seats provided for an audience that did not exist.

As Banks scanned his surroundings, he realized he was completely alone. The once bustling grand hall had emptied in a blink of an eye. Suddenly, a voice from behind him caught him off guard, calling out his name. Turning around, he saw a ghostly figure in a finely tailored three-piece suit.

"I will be your defense in this matter," the ghost said, his voice oozing with confidence.

Banks was taken aback in surprise, "Defense? What are you talking about?"

"This is the trial, sonny," the ghost replied suavely. "And it is an actual trial, presided over by the god of death himself. You will be judged by the devil as the prosecutor, to determine if you are worthy to proceed to the afterlife."

Banks nodded uncertainly, still trying to grasp the situation.

"Excellent. Time is of the essence, we must proceed," the ghost urged him, leading him to his seat. As they made their way down the aisle, Banks noticed a sinister-looking figure with red skin, black horns, and bat-like wings staring back at him. It was the devil, the prosecutor. Now did he recognize, with clarity, the hall in which he stood. It was a courtroom. The god of death sat on the judge's bench, a witness stand beside him, the jury on the bleacher-like rows of seats, the benches behind them for an audience that remained deserted, and a prosecution and defendant's table.

As soon as Banks took his seat at the defendant's table, the seat uncomfortable and creaked sonorously when he sat down, the god of death slammed what appeared to be a gavel and spoke in a terrifying, gravelly voice that reverberated through the hall. "The court is now in session. The Devil versus Banks, the defendant. Banks is accused of unworthiness and impurity and is thus denied entry into further trials. How do you plead?"

Banks trembled in fear as the weight of the situation hit him. He felt as though he was on trial for his very existence, which it very well might be. He had died, then got on board this train on a chaotic ride, then now he was in a trial. His head hurt just thinking about how that worked.

The courtroom was silent as Bank's lawyer spoke confidently, "My client, Jonathan Weatherby Banks, pleads not guilty, Your Honor. We will prove he is good in life and shall pass onto the next trial."

The god of death replied, "Very well, the prosecution may begin."

The devil rose from his seat, grinning mockingly as he bowed to the jury and said, "Your Honor and the jury, Mr. Banks stands accused of impurity and unworthiness. He is evil in his life and should be sentenced to the fires of hell, where he shall burn eternally. I will prove beyond a reasonable doubt that Banks is guilty."

Bank's lawyer interrupted swiftly with confidence, "Your Honor and the jury, my client is innocent. We will prove he is not guilty."

The god of death commanded, "The prosecution may call witnesses to the stand."

The devil waved his hand and in an instant, Bank's dead grandfather appeared in his spectral form. Banks was surprised, shocked even, and delighted to see his grandfather again so spontaneously, but he soon realized his grandfather was there to testify against him, not for him. When he was alive, his grandfather, when his parents were frequently busy, raised him and cared for him, and now his ghost was here to testify against him. A mix of emotions slammed into Banks, including fear and betrayal.

"I call to the stand Mr. Banks' grandfather," the devil said.

"Barnabus Banks." the god of death said, his voice echoing throughout the chamber. "Do you swear to tell the truth, the whole truth, and nothing but the truth?"

"I do," Barnabus said.

"So, Barnabus. Did Jonathan get into trouble in school?" the devil asked.

Banks' heart dropped as he recalled his troubling school days. His grandfather replied monotonously, almost as if he was possessed, "Yes."

"Objection!" Bank's lawyer cried out, "Petty things done in school do not restrict my client's access to the other trials."

"Silence!" the god of death hissed, his raspy, gravelly tone barely a whisper, but yet causing the room to fall into a perpetual reticence. "The prosecution may continue."

Bank's life flashed before his eyes, every insignificant and significant moment passing through his soul. Fear crept into him as he realized he could not recall any significant violations of the seven deadly sins, and he did not fancy burning in the fires of hell.

"Mr. Banks, do you recall that one time on a school trip when Jonathan attempted to climb on the skywalk?" the devil asked.

"Yes," his grandfather said.

"Your client here did lots of things in school, you know. Lots of letters were sent home. Tell me, Barnabus. Did the defendant do all these things? Let's see," the devil grinned maniacally. "He, snuck into the girl's bathroom, vandalized school property, did lots of swearing, never handed in any homework, lots of fighting too, inappropriate comments, covered the bathroom in mayonnaise-"

Bank's heart sank to the bottom of the metaphoric ocean. All these things suddenly played back in his head like an old film in a theater, as clear as day. Every single memory. Was he going to burn eternally for doing these things he thought were harmless pranks and mucking around? Dread and despair started consuming him, circulating through his veins and sending him shaking with panic. He shuddered to think what 'burning eternally' would be like.

"That's enough." The god of death brought his gavel down with a sonorous *bang.* The defense may now cross-examine the witness."

Bank's lawyer stood up, shaking his head, annoyed, and asked, "With every single one of my clients you do this. They are ordinary, good men, and deserve every right to pass onto the afterlife. He has had a normal, albeit boring life until his unfortunate demise. Unless some real criminals pass through here, stop trying to accuse them of random, petty things. Unless my client has really committed a major violation of the sins, he is allowed to pass through."

His grandfather shook his head. "No. He has not."

The devil opened his mouth, perhaps to deliver a counter-remark, when he was cut off at once by the gravelly voice of the god of death, "We may now move on to the closing arguments."

The devil readjusted his lips and said, "Members of the jury. Today, you have heard testimony from Barnabus Banks, the defendant's grandfather. Jonathan Banks has clearly committed crimes that deny his entry into the trials and, consequently, the afterlife."

Bank's lawyer replied at once without a moment's hesitation. It was clear that this ghost was very experienced in his trade. "Jonathan Banks has hardly done anything resembling a crime. He has all but done harmless things in his naive childhood and at school, which might I add, at that stage he has not had a full grasp on the nature of human life, and that is why he shall be granted access to the afterlife. Every soul that passes through here is almost every single time, innocent. Stop trying to drag innocent souls into the fires of hell, you scornful being. You just want more singers in your 'orchestra' of people screaming in pain. Find an actual sinner to sentence. The jury, please find the defendant not guilty. Thank you."

The devil snarled at them, his expression turned to one of anger.

The god of death finally said, "Members of the jury, you have heard all of the testimony concerning this case. It is now up to you to determine the facts. You and you alone, are the judges of the fact. In just a moment, you may proceed to the jury room to consider your verdict. One of the first things you will want to do is to select a foreperson that will preside over your deliberations the way that a chairperson does at a meeting. It will be the foreperson's duty to sign the verdict form when you have agreed on a verdict. Whatever verdict you render must be unanimous. That is each and every person must agree on the same verdict. You may now go to the deliberation room."

The jury vanished into nothingness at once, so suddenly it made Banks jump in surprise. Perhaps the way they get into the deliberation room was by teleportation.

The silence that followed was unnerving and harrowing, at least to Banks. It seemed to last for an eternity as the room was so muted he would've heard a fly land on a surface. He doubted that his lawyer's argument and cross-examine would do anything to tip the odds in his favor. Were the jury going to decide in favor of the prosecutor? Was he going to burn in fire forever? Butterflies, no, crows flew around in his stomach. Although he did not think a ghost would sweat, fountains of liquid started flowing down his forehead. His dead heart beat wildly, jumping and thrashing uncontrollably.

Bank's lawyer, who had by now noticed his client shaking in fear like a tree in a tropical storm, placed his ghostly hand on his shoulder. "Relax. You'll be fine. Trust me, every soul who passed through here did something the devil points fingers at and exaggerates. Unless a serial killer of some master crook comes through they all pass through. Stop shaking. Calm yourself, hon." The confidence and certainty in his voice managed to halt Bank's shaking, although his teeth still clattered as if he was freezing. He became more assured, however, the evil glee the devil gave to him provided him with more doubts.

After a long and painful silence, the jury appeared back in their seats.

The god of death asked, "Has the jury reached a verdict?"

"Your Honor, we have," croaked the foreperson of the spectral jury. The raspiness in his voice betrayed a bone-dry throat as if he had just crossed the scorching desert. "After a thorough consideration of the evidence presented, we find the defendant, Jonathan Banks, not guilty."

"Thank you for your service," the god of death said. "Court is adjourned." He banged his gavel and vanished in a puff of smoke, leaving not a single trace behind that might have suggested he was even there.

His lawyer flashed him a grin, and the devil roared in fury, vexed by the verdict. He stood up, giving the defendants one last, raging glance before dissipating into nothingness himself. It seemed that beings in the underworld have a tendency to simply teleport or disappear away. Banks himself let loose a huge sigh of relief, all his breath exiting out of his mouth in alleviation. He turned to give his thanks to his lawyer, but before he could catch another breath, the room in front of him suddenly evaporated into nothingness. His grandfather, the god, his lawyer, and the jury were all gone. He instead found himself standing in front of the dilapidated, worn train station once again where the Midnight Express now appeared, looking as old but yet magnificent as ever, steam billowing out of its chimney.

The conductor made his presence known as the front coach's door swung open with a flourish. "Well, what are you waiting for?" he asked with a sense of urgency. "You have passed the trial, and we must now make haste to reach the afterlife. Time is of the essence!"

Banks looked around the station, his experience after passing away had been an odd one, to say the least. Why couldn't he have never passed away in the first place? He would be back home, sleeping in his bed, then waking up the next morning, going downstairs, and tearing open the fresh box of cereal. Then he could go to work, but what work? His sickness had made him unable to work at all. Banks realized that after the trial, now he must come to terms with death and how he could probably never visit the living world again as a ghost. Hey, perhaps he could see his grandfather in the afterlife. After all, he's dead as well. Onward to the afterlife, whatever that may be. It was difficult to fathom that Banks had once pondered about what happens after death, and now here he was, experiencing it firsthand. Banks had been picked up by a ghost train, went on a wild ride to the underworld, faced trial with the bloody devil as his prosecutor, won, and now he was back again, facing the Midnight Express.

He stepped into the coach and took a seat, joining the other souls who had also passed the trial. The shrill whistle of the train sounded once again, a sound that somehow he had become all too familiar with, despite only being on the train once. The engine started to crawl forward, and they soon found themselves cruising along the darkness of the underworld at a moderate pace.

The journey was calm in the void of the underworld. Banks peered out of the windows, but all he could see was darkness and an endless expanse of it. Without any landscape to gauge their progress, he couldn't be sure they were making any headway at all. However, the loud chugging of the locomotive and the hissing of steam escaping from the chimney suggested otherwise. The dim lanterns hanging from the coach's ceiling were the only source of light in the barren darkness. Banks soon drifted off to sleep, only to be abruptly awoken by an announcement from the conductor.

"We are now approaching the afterlife. This will be your final destination. Please prepare to disembark."

Banks peered out of the window again and was surprised to see a light source amongst the blackness for the first time in the form of a luminous, blinding light in the distance. He assumed that this was the entrance to the afterlife. As he braced himself for what was to come, Banks couldn't help but feel a sense of trepidation. He had lived a short life, yet he felt it was a very fulfilling life, and he sat, ready to move on to the next chapter of his existence. The express suddenly picked up speed, hurtling towards the glow. The clanging and chugging of the wheels grew louder, and the hissing of steam became a deafening roar as they raced toward the light. Banks' eyes were blinded by the sudden golden glow as they sped into it head-on, departing for a new world.

His eyes were then almost forced open and he found himself in a new world of pure, blinding light. It took him several moments to adjust to the pure radiance he was now in. He felt the dazzling light pierce through the coaches' windows. This realm starkly contrasted with the underworld, which was filled with darkness and an empty void. Here, it was bright, sparkling with light and beauty. As the harsh rays struck Bank's eyes, he felt all his worries and anxieties wash away. So this was the afterlife, a haven of pure light and serenity and tranquillity. A place where you are truly at peace. Although there seemed to be nothing but light in the afterlife, he still felt happy, instead of the usual feeling of emptiness.

The train let loose a high whistle as it steadily slowed to a halt. The coach's doors swung open automatically by magic. Banks got up from his seat and exited the carriage into a new life.

The Post-It Puzzle

* * *

Recently, I had the privilege of venturing to the illustrious city of London for my tertiary education. Though my ambition was to attend Cambridge, the institution, King's College London, I had been accepted to was more than adequate to provide me with an outstanding education to fortify my future prospects.

However, the on-campus dormitories were extravagantly priced, to put it mildly. Nevertheless, my father had an old acquaintance, who resided and worked in River Street, a mere 20-minute tube ride away from campus. He generously offered to accommodate me in exchange for a helping hand with his work.

Upon my arrival at Number 7, River Street, I was uncertain of what to expect. As my father had informed me, it was the abode and workplace of Dr. Julius Collmore. However, it did not resemble a medical clinic or a place where a doctor would conduct their practice. It was a quaint, sand-colored brick house with a charming oak door.

It was not long before I learned that Dr. Collmore was not a medical doctor but simply had earned a Ph.D. in various subjects. His expertise was in providing private investigator services, and he ran his own company, aptly named Collmore Investigations.

"In simple terms," he described to me, "I get called when someone wants to either dig up some dirt on someone or investigate something to do with money. Those are the most common cases. One I get a lot is someone accusing another of infidelity."

I have decided, after some thought, to take up my pen and write down a small adventure and mishap that has occurred with my stay with the doctor.

* * *

The work assigned to me by the doctor was monotonous and dreary. During my educational hiatus, he deemed it fit to inundate me with a plethora of paperwork. The reality of private investigation work did not live up to the glamorous image I had conjured up of spying on others or sneaking into all sorts of places. Instead, I spent most of my time filing case reports and undertaking insipid research. However, the most odious part of the job was the fact that I had unwittingly assumed the role of the doctor's housekeeper, on top of my other responsibilities. I was responsible for tidying up his living quarters and workspace, in addition to preparing his morning tea and breakfast. Regrettably, this also involved the less savory task of cleaning the bathroom.

The genesis of my adventure began on a Saturday morning. I woke up early at around 8 AM, normally well before Collmore, who was not known for being an early riser. I did not expect, however, to see him already ensconced in his office, clad in a nightgown, and speaking into the landline.

He interrupted his conversation and said, "Good morning, Jack! I have some work to attend to early on. Could you make me some coffee, eggs, and bacon, please?" before returning to his phone call. I was still not too keen on the idea of serving as his housekeeper/butler, but I begrudgingly made my way to the kitchen and started the coffee maker. I cracked open two eggs and retrieved the container of bacon from the refrigerator. I proceeded to pour oil into a frying pan and heat it up when Collmore stormed into the kitchen, now changed into a grey coat and brown fedora, and demanded, "Forget about the eggs and bacon. We need something quicker. Pour the coffee into the thermos and let's go."

"Is there a particular reason we have to leave so early in the morning?" I inquired.

"A client," he replied candidly.

The doctor instructed me to change my attire expeditiously,

and in the meantime, he proceeded to enter the pantry-room, emerging after a few minutes with two pots of cup noodles. I opened the lid and began to consume the warm, salty broth.

"Surely, you realize, as delicious as they are, cup noodles do not qualify as a nutritious breakfast option?" I queried.

"Indeed, my dear colleague, but desperate times call for desperate measures, and the rapidity with which one can devour these morsels is an undeniable advantage," he retorted with a chuckle in his unnecessary linguistic flair. "Now, let us hasten. We have a pressing matter to attend to."

Moments later, we were en route to our destination, cruising through the bustling streets of London in the doctor's sleek Prius. Despite my earlier admonishments, the doctor was slurping away at his pot of noodles as he navigated the vehicle. Curiosity piqued, I implored him as to the nature of our mission and why it necessitated such urgency.

"We have received a call from a client with an urgent matter to attend to. You didn't forget to bring your notepad, Mr. Scott, did you?" he reminded me.

"But, couldn't this have waited until later in the day?" I pressed.

"My dear fellow, impatience is one of my character traits," he replied with a grin.

"Very well. What is the nature of this case?" I inquired.

"I shall let our new client provide the details," he responded.

Upon arrival, we found ourselves in front of a modest abode situated in the London suburbs, its brick facade identical to the row of connected houses it was part of. The narrow street was congested with parked vehicles, as the city began to stir awake with the rising sun casting a warm, orange hue upon the buildings. Dr. Collmore parked the car and we proceeded to the door, where we were greeted by a middle-aged man with a fiery mane, clad in a t-shirt and shorts, despite the frigid November weather.

Introductions were exchanged, and our host, a Mr. Walter Carill, escorted us to his bedroom. The bed, disheveled and unmade, was tucked away in a corner, while a wooden desk from IKEA was situated in the opposite corner, next to a desktop computer. A profusion of Post-It notes adorned the desk, bearing scrawled and scribbled reminders in almost indecipherable handwriting, such as 'Clean toilet' and 'Sweep floor.' Mr. Carill's voice quivered with fear as he relayed the bizarre situation to me.

"Mr. Scott, Post-It notes have been manifesting themselves throughout my home, and I swear I have not written them! They materialize out of thin air, all around my house in unrecognizable handwriting! I've not told anyone about my chores, and I have had no visitors, yet they show up out of nowhere!"

The doctor instructed me to document his every word as he interviewed Mr. Carill, and he meticulously examined every inch of the house, presumably searching for any clues that may shed light on this baffling situation.

After 30 minutes, he announced that our work was done. "I have collected all the necessary evidence. I will email Mr. Carill about the matter of payment, and we shall depart now," the doctor declared.

During the journey back to River Street, I inquired about the evidence he had uncovered.

"A few fingerprints," he replied, his tone heavy with confusion. "That corresponds to Carill's own when I took his prints, that makes sense as he would've touched them. I examined the ink on the Post-It Notes and did a small ink-analysis and test. The ink corresponds to one of Carill's pens, which I suppose the perpetrator used to write it, but then Carill himself would have written them. No evidence other than that. However, Mr. Carill claims to be unaware of the source of these notes. This is a perplexing case."

"Do you think he is being dishonest?" I queried.

"If he is, then he is an incredibly skilled actor to feign such fear. Furthermore, I cannot imagine a reason why he would expend his resources on such a prank. I believe him to be truthful, Mr. Scott," the doctor asserted.

The most bizarre occurrence took place the following day. After breakfast, I began to experience severe discomfort, suffering from excruciating headaches, abdominal pain, and muscle aches. It was like I'd caught the flu.

Though not a medical practitioner, the doctor possessed enough expertise to procure medication from the nearest pharmacy. I was confined to bed for several days. The doctor entertained the notion that my illness was connected to the case of the inexplicable Post-It notes. As a highly organized individual, he maintained meticulous records of our movements, including my own. I had not left River Street on the day we visited Carill's house, so my illness was most likely related to that visit. However, Carill had not reported any flu-like symptoms, and his influenza test was negative, and so was mine.

The doctor donned PPE and made several visits to Carill's home to investigate my illness, convinced that my ailment was linked to the investigation. I, on the other hand, believed it was merely a coincidence. Nonetheless, the doctor was dismissive of my point of view.

After five days, I recovered and resumed my duties as the doctor's housekeeper and assistant engaging in monotonous paperwork on his laptop. Sometimes I considered persuading my father to pay for a dormitory instead of working as someone's housekeeper.

We returned to Carill's abode a few days later. The doctor instructed him to install a surveillance camera to monitor the premises non-stop for any strange occurrences that may take place. The following day, we came back to assess the footage, only to find the recordings folder empty, despite the camera being in operation the entire time. When questioned about the issue, Carill claimed to have no recollection of anything at all. The matter was highly perplexing and left me utterly bewildered.

Within a week, Carill contacted the doctor again to report another peculiar incident. Following a hearty meal of chicken curry from the local Asian diner, the doctor drove us to Carill's residence. While Carill shared his diary with me, the doctor conducted a second inspection of the house. The diary was a small, leather-bound notebook with a pen holder on the side that contained a petite blue ballpoint pen. The handwriting inside was immaculate, documenting Carill's daily routine from January until the present. However, the recent entries were a chaotic mess of unintelligible scribbles and scrawls. One entry, in particular, had been crossed out, and beneath it, more indecipherable text was scrawled. Strangely enough, Carill denied having written in the diary since our previous visit, because the doctor had told me that in the ink test he had just conducted on the kitchen table, the ink corresponded to Carill's pen, the same one that wrote the Post-It notes, which only added to the already bizarre situation. The doctor surmised that these developments could be connected to the enigmatic Post-It notes.

I snapped several photographs of the diary and made note of the increasing number of Post-It notes scattered around the room, each bearing more incomprehensible handwriting. Carill had even relocated from his bedroom to the living room out of fear. As I sat on the couch downstairs, waiting for the doctor to complete his examination, I found myself contemplating the origin of the Post-It notes and the scribbles in the diary. It was undoubtedly an enigma.

Carill claimed that he was the only individual with access to the property, and the reinforced door locks showed no signs of forced entry. He had refused any and all claims that he had written them himself. Although it was not a plausible explanation my only conclusion was that the disturbance was either caused by a specter or an intruder breaking into the premises.

A few moments elapsed before the doctor completed his examination, and we all awaited his response with holding our breath in anticipation.

"Have you made any discoveries, Doctor?" Carill asked, wringing his hands nervously, his voice shaking with fear.

"Regrettably, Mr. Carill, I have formulated several theories, but none of them appears to be valid or relevant to the situation. The evidence is also perplexing. You claim to have not written in your diary or composed the Post-It notes, but yet the ink tests and fingerprinting points to you." the doctor replied in a somber tone.

"But I swear on God's name, I did not do anything which you accuse me of! My house is haunted! What am I supposed to do?" Carill cried out in distress.

"Please be patient, Mr. Carill. Allow me a few more days to investigate further. We should locate the perpetrator," the doctor suggested, attempting to comfort the trembling homeowner.

And so, we departed from the haunted house and returned to River Street. The doctor appeared to be just as perplexed as the rest of us, as he announced that he required time to ponder the situation. He retired to his garage, where his Toyota Prius was parked outside, and a large table covered in Lego pieces occupied the rest of the space. The doctor confided in me that constructing objects out of plastic bricks aided his cognitive processes. Meanwhile, I occupied myself by tidying the living room and watching television.

The following day was a brief hiatus from the current case, as a couple arrived for a short consultation. While the doctor conducted the interview, I made detailed notes regarding the particulars of their case.

After the couple had left, I ascended the stairs to immerse myself in a good book. Halfway through a chapter, a cry of "EUREKA!" from the doctor downstairs disrupted my reading. I heard a flurry of footsteps and the doctor rushed upstairs, reminiscent of the Greek mathematician Archimedes who famously ran out of his bath naked and into the streets to proclaim his discovery to the king.

Puzzled by the doctor's excitement, I asked, "What is it?"

"I have figured it out!" the doctor exclaimed with fervor.

"Figured out what?" I queried, my curiosity piqued.

"We must leave immediately!" the doctor declared with urgency. Without further explanation, he rushed out the door and into his Prius. I followed him reluctantly, wondering what could have prompted yet another sudden departure.

Twenty minutes later, we arrived at Carill's doorstep. What caught my attention was the doctor's insistence on us both wearing gas masks, which struck me as very odd. When Carill answered the doorbell, the doctor announced that he had solved the case and instructed him to put on a gas mask as well. Carill complied with the doctor's request, and we proceeded to the living room, where the doctor began to explain his theory.

"This case has confounded me more than any other I have encountered, but I believe I have finally solved this conundrum," the doctor stated with confidence. "First, let me prove my hypothesis."

He produced a screwdriver and approached the carbon monoxide detector on the kitchen ceiling. After unscrewing the detector, he removed its batteries and replaced them with fresh ones from his pocket, then screwed them back on.

Immediately, a shrill and deafening alarm erupted from the detector, causing me to gasp and instinctively cover my ears, but to no avail. The doctor had to unscrew the detector and forcibly remove the batteries to silence the blaring siren.

After a brief moment of silence, Carill broke the stillness. "There's carbon monoxide in my house! Run-"

"Yes, we are quite aware of that," the doctor interjected. "This confirms my hypothesis and produces a conclusive result. Allow me to explain."

The doctor continued swiftly on, "Your carbon monoxide detector had run out of battery, and when CO gas permeated your home, it was unable to detect the harmful gas. Carbon monoxide induces amnesia and makes you forget the most critical of things, and yet still think it is perfectly fine. You wrote the Post-It notes yourself to remind yourself of things as you keep forgetting to do your matters, and eventually forgot you even made the notes, and even your own handwriting on the Post-It Notes as you somehow had an entirely new handwriting almost every day because you kept forgetting the last one. This is backed up by the evidence directed to your pen and your fingerprints, proving you wrote the notes yourself. You erased all the footage from the camera you set up because there was nothing suspicious to see. You were intending to inform me of your amnesia, but you simply forgot. And when Jack here returned and fell ill, his symptoms were consistent with carbon monoxide poisoning."

The doctor paused for a moment before continuing, "And that is why I instructed you to wear a gas mask. Mr. Carill, I recommend that you replace your carbon monoxide detector and notify the fire department as soon as possible."

And that is how Dr. Julius Collmore solved what I dubbed the 'Post-It Puzzle'. On the drive back to River Street, I asked the doctor how he had arrived at the conclusion of carbon monoxide poisoning. His response was a modest, "Well, I suppose the idea just occurred to me."

The Plight Of The Nicholas

* * *

CHAPTER I

In the distant future, Arthur stood at the plasma window, gazing out into the seemingly infinite expanse of space before him. Initially, he was thrilled at the prospect of embarking on a long-distance voyage, but he soon realized that the reality of the situation was quite dull and drab. It was a diplomatic mission to a solar system at the edge of the Milky Way, and even faster-than-light travel would take 20+ years. To make matters worse, the Hypersleep cells were only partially operational, allowing them to slumber for a mere 13 years. Until repairs were made, they were forced to endure 7 arduous years on the ship. While they could activate the hyperspeed function, a cutting-edge piece of technology utilizing wormholes to expedite their journey, their extensive travels necessitated the conservation of fuel, and a hyperspeed jump required most of their reserves.

Arthur harbored a strong resentment toward Captain Sents, holding him accountable for their current predicament. The Captain had opted to cut costs on this expedition, commissioning a below-average, second-hand vessel without a power generator. Despite Arthur's repeated attempts to raise the issue with the Captain, he skillfully evaded discussion and deflected responsibility.

Arthur was tending to the fuel tanks when the ship's bell rang throughout the speakers. Subsequently, Sents' voice echoed over the intercom, calling for all crew members to report to the bridge, announcing the sighting of a pirate ship.

Arthur's heart nearly stopped as he listened to the announcement. His stomach churned with anxiety at the thought of encountering a pirate vessel. After mustering up the courage to move, he laboriously trudged through the winding corridors toward the bridge, entering the elevator and ascending to the bridge. Ever since the discovery of advanced space travel and the Second Space Race, pirates have plagued the galaxy, pillaging ships and stealing their goods. He hoped they wouldn't be their next target.

When he arrived on the bustling bridge, the cacophony of sounds assaulted his ears. His colleagues feverishly worked the numerous panels of switches and levers that controlled the ship. Captain Sents himself sat at the pilot's station, furiously typing into the onboard computer and flicking levers. Next to the pilot's station hung a Union Jack, displaying their allegiance and country. The atmosphere was frenzied with screaming and shouting.

"Attention C4, report your status immediately!"

A tense voice barked through the intercom, cutting through the ruckus that had enveloped the spaceship. The suddenness of the call jolted everyone on board, causing them to pause in their tasks and look toward the speaker.

The response was swift and urgent, "Pirate vessel detected, approaching our sector with coordinates 10, 10, 30, 809, 5006, 0!"

The gravity of the situation was palpable as the crew scrambled to prepare for a potential battle. The captain wasted no time in giving orders, "Copy that, Sans. Arm the guns and ready the ship for hyperspeed. Increase fuel speed to the maximum."

"But our fuel-"

"We don't need to worry about that for now," Sents barked.

But their worst fears were confirmed when a crew member cried out, "Sir! The pirate ship has opened its gunports!"

Arthur's heart sank. Their peaceful expedition had turned into a nightmare as they now faced a ship of pirates intent on battling and pillaging them. The prospect of combat was not something he had anticipated nor desired.

"All hands to battle stations!" Sents commanded his voice quivering with a mixture of fear and urgency. "Prepare for hyperspeed boosters, quickly!"

The ship was now a hive of frantic activity as the crew moved with purpose, their movements synchronized in preparation for the impending attack. The sound of footsteps, clanging metal, and mechanical whirring filled the air, creating a cacophony of chaos.

Arthur was startled by the sudden bark of a crew member, "What are you doing there, boy? Don't just stand there! Adjust the hyperspeed gear and increase the ship's helm sensitivity to 200% immediately! Move, you idiot!"

His legs moved without conscious thought, and he found himself at the controls, cranking the handle to the appropriate level. His fingers trembled as he did so, his mind racing with thoughts of what might happen next.

A voice crackled over the intercom, but before the message could be conveyed, a massive jolt shook the ship violently. Arthur was thrown across the room, his body slamming against a steel wall. Pain seared through his head, and he groaned in agony. The captain was flung off his chair, and a co-pilot crashed into a plasma screen displaying the engine heat.

"Captain!" The intercom crackled with a sense of urgency. "Our hyperspeed engines have been hit!"

Sents swore under his breath, his face contorted with frustration.

Arthur's heart sank as the realization hit him that their means of escape had been destroyed. The loss of their hyperspeed engines meant they were now stranded and vulnerable. Fear gripped him, sending chills down his spine.

"Captain, orders!" said the same voice on the intercom.

"Open fire. Now!" Sents roared.

Nicholas's guns opened fire, and through the windows, he could see plasma bolts connecting to the pirate cruiser. Fireballs exploded on the cruiser, causing damage. The pirates returned fire and the *Nicholas* was hit hard.

"Boy! Adjust engine gear to 200% and crank fuel usage to no limit and maximum efficiency!" Sents ordered.

"What? That's-"

"Shut up. I'm going to jump to hyperspeed. Go!"

"But sir!" The co-pilot said. "The hyperspeed engines-"

"I don't give a bloody damn about the engines! Under the right setting, we'll force a jump to hyperspeed if we output enough speed. Now, boy, get to work!" Sents roared.

"Sir!" Arthur shouted. "The engines'll explode-"

"I DON'T GIVE A DAMN, I SAID!"

"But captain, the engines will explode!" One of the crewmembers piped in.

"THEY WON'T IF WE REGULATE IT AND HOLD IT STEADY NOW BLOODY GET TO WORK OR I'LL BLOODY EJECT YOU LIKE THE DEAD WEIGHT YOU ARE!" Sents barked.

Arthur shuddered at the captain's wrath and got to work, praying the engines won't explode and send them spiraling into space.

Meanwhile, outside, a furious battle was taking place. Plasma bolts and missiles were flying everywhere, exploding left and right and causing damage. From the pirate ship, the hangar bay opened, and outcome a squadron of fighter jets shot toward the *Nicholas.*

That was a problem. The jets were moving too fast for *Nicholas's* auto-aim system to keep up and so the guns simply ignored the jets and continued firing on the enemy ship as the jets flew around the ship and harassed them by flying around the ship like flies, dropping bombs everywhere.

Sents' voice came up on the intercom again. "Everyone, brace yourselves, we will be jumping to hyperspeed, I repeat, jumping to hyperspeed, since the hyperspeed engines are down we will be forcing a jump, please brace for impact."

Arthur watched in horror as Sents ignored all the warnings that trying to jump to hyperspeed without the correct engine will end up with an overheated engine or even make it explode. He furiously adjusted the controls.

"Brace for impact! Check all requirements, make sure engine is regulated, full thrust, coordinates in place, Hyperspeed in 3, 2, 1–"

And so he flicked the lever. And so, as predicted, the ship proceeded to explode.

Even at the bridge, Arthur felt the heatwave that enveloped *Nicholas.* The roaring engines at the back of the ship roared at full thrust. A crewmember had forced it to go beyond its maximum speed with the fuel they had, overriding the circuits. The *Nicholas* lurched forward like a choking man for a split second, and then the engines and rockets exploded. The engines seemed to split apart and turn into dust and a fireball erupted from it like a volcanic eruption.

It did not help that a plasma bolt from the pirate cruiser had just hit the ship, causing another explosion.

Sents roared and cursed. Arthur sighed.

Well, perhaps, perhaps on the positive side of things, the pirate cruiser saw the engines exploding as their victory, and it changed course in the opposite direction and steered away.

CHAPTER II

After the calamity, the surviving crew members were far from pleased with Sents' actions. He had tried to hail potential rescuers through the functional communicators, but to no avail. The mayday communicator was non-functional, rendering all other communication equipment useless. With the radar as the only operational equipment, they found themselves defenseless, waiting for their supplies of food, water, and oxygen to run out. The ship was becalmed, dead in space.

Moreover, the crew's morale was at rock bottom. The dejected and dispirited personnel were slumped in the corner, wallowing in self-pity and anticipating their inevitable demise. Sents, who had sealed himself off in his quarters, had not been checked on by anyone. The sleeping quarters were a very gloomy place. Some were mourning the loss of their comrades, others tried to cheer themselves up by playing cards or using the old console on board and the 1 racing game they had.

Subsequently, a group of individuals discovered that one of the escape pods had been unscathed, and they availed themselves of this opportunity, fleeing into the unknown, and leaving everyone else behind. This blatant betrayal had only exacerbated the already abysmal morale.

The only individual who remained resolute in his conviction that there was still hope was Arthur. Utilizing the last remaining battery power of the ship's computer, he activated the radar, which proved to be more useful than expected. Most ships were registered on the GPS and the radar, including the pirate cruiser, which he successfully pinpointed. Since the cruiser was a large vessel, it could not move very rapidly, and as a result, he found it in the neighboring sector without much difficulty.

Arthur had devised an audacious plan to board the pirate cruiser, hijack it, and then fly it back to the Nicholas using one of the smaller, undamaged aircraft from an unexplored hangar bay. Despite being an extremely risky and reckless undertaking, he was determined to carry out his plan. However, he refrained from sharing his scheme with anyone because he knew that Sents would hinder his efforts. Sents had a history of being hypocritical and disdainful towards Arthur due to his youth and solitary nature. He had been his crewmember in a previous mission, a failure that resulted in the loss of his wealth. He blamed Arthur, although he had nothing to do with it. Perhaps it was because he was the youngest member of the crew, and he assumed he made lots of mistakes. Although he recognized that he could benefit from having additional crew members, he could not bring himself to trust them. No, this would be a solo endeavor. '

Thus, Arthur set his plan in motion. One night, after everyone fell asleep, he covertly left his quarters, grabbed his rucksack, which he had packed earlier in preparation for this mission, and a pistol that he had appropriated from the armory in case of emergency. He silently made his way to the hangar bay where the old, dilapidated freighter, the STS Artemis, was kept. It was a neglected and dusty hunk that had been forgotten by the previous owner. As he approached it, he could smell, from a distance, the dust and the dry, cardboard-like smell that radiated from the ship. As he hauled open the doors, it revealed an interior that looked like it had seen far better days, with ripped furniture, cracked walls, and lights that kept flickering on and off. It was also poorly ventilated, and as soon as he stepped inside, he felt his lungs gasping for air as the interior was devoid of any oxygen. He rushed to turn on the ventilators and air supplies, which were old, torn pieces of equipment that played a strange buzzing noise whenever they were on. However it was still operational, and that was all that mattered. He boarded the Artemis and began the ignition sequence. The ancient engine, clearly already stressed simply by the ignition sequence, groaned and creaked, emitting sonorous sounds that can be heard even from the cockpit. When the lever didn't work, he had to use a screwdriver to pry open the hatch into the engine room and manually jiggle the mechanisms until it eventually roared to life, and when it did, let loose an unpleasant gas that had him gagging back to the cockpit. He sat back down on the pilot's seat and took off.

* * *

When Arthur was eventually discovered to be missing, he had already set off on his intrepid journey aboard the *Artemis*. He had ingeniously recorded and saved the tracking data and GPS coordinates of the pirate cruiser onto a Universal Portable Storage device, and deftly installed it into the Artemis's onboard computer. From that point on, his focus was unwaveringly fixed on pursuing the gargantuan cruiser, but he was faced with numerous challenges along the way.

Initially, he encountered difficulties in steering the *Artemis*. Although he was accustomed to piloting smaller vessels such as starfighters and shuttles, the *Artemis* was of an entirely different scale. Its size was overwhelming, and its wear and tear meant that it was anything but nimble. As a solo pilot in a ship meant for at least a copilot and pilot, he had to contend with operating multiple switches, levers, and joysticks simultaneously, making it an arduous task to maneuver the ship. Moreover, the ship's unsteady condition made the task even more daunting.

As if that wasn't enough, the next hurdle he faced was activating the hyperspeed function. This endeavor was fraught with peril, and Arthur's apprehension was palpable. After configuring the hyperspeed course using the Navcom and hoping that it was still operational, the sudden jolt of extreme acceleration caused him to lose his breath. The gravity of the situation was amplified by the fact that he had failed to remember the existence of hyperspeed-resistant seatbelts that protected you from the tremendous speed and acceleration. Consequently, he was flung out of his seat, the seat belts snapped like twigs, and he was violently propelled against a wall, giving him a few small wounds.

He had hoped to employ the autopilot function to steer through the hyperspeed tunnel, but the *Artemis* was no high-end space-craft, and the autopilot was inoperable. Therefore, he was left with no other option but to manually steer the ship, a feat which proved to be more than a little challenging.

When Arthur finally emerged from the tumultuous hyperspeed travel, he was greeted with the formidable sight of the pirate cruiser. It was an imposing behemoth, with its metallic exterior gleaming menacingly in the darkness of space. At this moment, Arthur knew that he had to accomplish what he had set out to do. With unwavering determination, he increased the speed of the Artemis, but upon approaching the cruiser, he decreased the velocity drastically and meticulously crept up towards it.

CHAPTER III

When Arthur examined the *Artemis*, it revealed to him that it was heavily equipped with speed and stealth modifications. The engine was silent, well it used to be, but the mufflers had long been damaged. And speaking of the engines, it was clear someone had attached extra racing-grade boosters, a jacked-up hyperspeed engine, and an advanced stealth emitter. Thus, he planned to board the cruiser slowly and covertly. Unfortunately, his intuition proved flawed as the cruiser immediately unleashed its weapon on him, sending him into a panic. He tried to avoid the incoming missiles, which narrowly missed him by executing a hard port maneuver.

The pirate ship did not stop at that, instead, it directed all its weapons at Arthur's ship. Its laser cannons were roaring to life, leaving Arthur bewildered about why they would consider him an enemy. Arthur had no idea of what was going on. Evasive maneuvers were his only way out of the situation, so he increased his speedometer to maximum and maneuvered the joystick with great skill, though that proved to be another mistake. This move sent the Artemis freighter shooting forward like a bullet, and Arthur's head collided with his seat, though it had the benefit of taking him out of range from the guns.

Now, Arthur had to figure out how to board the ship without getting blasted with the guns, plasma, lasers, missiles, and anything else thrown his way. He weighed the options of attempting to charge into the hangar by increasing the speed or trying to shoot his way out of the mess. The ship had a turret, which he maneuvered and set to auto-aim, hoping that the outdated hunker could still hit anything that moved.

Regrettably, the turret literally shot at *anything*, and blasted away uselessly at an asteroid, while Arthur's proximity alarm beeped. On checking the 360 view camera, he saw that the pirate cruiser had dispatched three starfighters, now speeding towards the Artemis. Arthur had to act fast to evade them. He turned the speedometer to the maximum and flipped up the weapons GUI screen. The ship's AI confirmed the target lock, and he fired at the starfighters, but they dodged at the last minute and opened fire on thc Artemis.

Arthur swerved the ship to dodge the incoming fire and eventually got a better view of the cruiser. He noticed a clear opening to an open hangar guarded by two sentry cannons. To enter the hangar, he had to take out the sentry cannons, tank the cannons with the maximum shield on the Artemis, and rush in. Arthur adjusted the engine boost and did a loop-the-loop behind the starfighters, immediately opening fire. One of the starfighters got hit and exploded, but the others managed to avoid the shots.

The starfighters split up, and Arthur chased after the one heading west, but in the corner of his eye, he saw the cruiser launch a tracking missile toward him. He cursed under his breath in frustration but was relieved when the turret aimbot locked onto the missile and destroyed it in a fireball.

The other starfighter behind him opened fire, causing a small explosion that shook the *Artemis*. Arthur juggled the joystick and dodged the plasma bolts, and the turret fired at the starfighter, forcing it to retreat. Arthur focused on the starfighter in front of him, which was extremely fast. They had a brief chase among several asteroids, both ships bobbing and weaving, but he eventually got a lock onto the fighter and released a missile, reducing it to space junk in an instant.

Arthur then turned tail and headed straight for the cruiser. The ship's guns were still firing, but he cranked up the shields to 100%, allowing him to take multiple hits before his engine sustained damage. Additionally, he jiggled 5% of the hyperspeed engine so that he could go even faster. He aimed the Artemis straight for the open hangar, enduring plasma bolts, missiles, and everything in between, shaking the *Artemis* like a boat in a heavy storm, as it bounced and lurched wildly, before by some miracle, managing to propel itself into the hangar-bay without exploding. Unfortunately, it was still at high speed and crashed straight into the wall of the hangar, which then bounced it toward the other one. He frantically tried to brake, but before he could it slammed into the other wall, jerking him violently. Arthur flicked the engine kill switch before it could crash further into the hangar and grabbed the lever to let down the landing gear. But he was way too slow. The ship instead, losing momentum, tumbled onto the ground, skidding vigorously, causing sparks to fly everywhere before eventually slowing to a halt.

Arthur let loose a huge sigh of relief and silently patted himself on the back for managing to accomplish that audacious maneuver. He took a swig from a jar of water, before shouldering his rucksack and opening the *Artemis*'s doors. He departed from the ship and into the large hangar, then started exploring the ship for some sort of way to hijack it.

* * *

Arthur quickly realized that the ship was predominantly managed by autonomous robots, rendering his job a lot less arduous. His expertise in all things related to computing was precisely what he needed to commandeer the vessel. By gaining control over the robots, he would possess complete control over the ship.

Stealthily and briskly, he scoured the ship's interiors. After a few minutes, he pinpointed a robot, shot it with his pistol, and rapidly hacked into its system. He procured an exclusive access code that enabled him to access the console room, the hivemind of the ship. Navigating his way through the corridors without being spotted, he finally arrived at the console room. The room was replete with rows of supercomputers and other high-tech equipment that served as the ship's nerve center.

Arthur whipped out a high-performance laptop and deftly plugged it into the console. He began to work his magic, breezing past the security protocols with ease. His next step was to hack into the main code and execute an override command. However, before he could accomplish his mission, the sound of the console room's door opening made him almost drop his laptop.

Reacting instinctively, he hastily unplugged his laptop, grabbed his pistol, and loaded it. The sound of an unfamiliar voice speaking in a thick accent made him startle. It was a human, not a robot. This meant that he had stumbled upon one of the few crew members on the ship.

Arthur muttered a curse under his breath. The footsteps he heard were partly robotic and partly human. This did not bode well for him. That meant the crewmember was most likely accompanied by security robots, most definitely armed. He was aware that he had nowhere to run, so he took refuge behind a towering supercomputer and readied himself, drawing his gun and resting his hand on the trigger.

"Come out now, intruder, whoever you are, before I have to shoot you! Well, I'll shoot you anyways, but will it be nice for you to come out so I don't have to look for you, y'know?" came a feminine voice, betraying an undercurrent of menace.

It was at this moment Arthur knew he was cornered with no escape.

CHAPTER IV

Arthur's mind raced as he pondered his next move. With danger lurking around every corner, he knew that he needed to act quickly if he was going to get out of this situation alive. Fortunately, he was a man with a plan.

Surveying the console room, Arthur spotted the perfect distraction: a supercomputer that he could use to sow confusion and create an opening to escape. Computers, when stressed, heat up. If he could turn off a module's cooling system and forced it to run many demanding programs, it would heat up and explode. With stealth and skill, he slipped towards the back of the room, his steps as silent as a cat's.

Once he reached his target, he quickly set to work. He plugged his trusty laptop into the supercomputer, using the access code he had obtained to gain entry. Then, he reached into his bag of tricks in his rucksack and pulled out a variety of spare parts, which he used to modify the computer to his liking. Finally, he wrote a custom script to create chaos within the system.

With a smirk of satisfaction, Arthur executed his plan. The supercomputer sprang to life with a loud hum, the fans whirring as the lines of code flashed across Arthur's screen. As he anticipated, the system began to lag, then overheat, smoke rising furiously. Arthur knew that it would be the perfect diversion to throw his pursuers off his trail.

He slid his homemade bomb-like device towards his foes, then quickly turned his attention to his safety and ducked, as a small explosion happened from the PC module he modified. A string of curses came in a foreign tongue. As he emerged from his hiding place to take a peek, he saw that the robots pursuing him were armed and ready for a fight. Without hesitation, he raised his pistol and opened fire, taking out the robots before they had a chance to retaliate.

Then, another shot rang out, striking one of the supercomputers and setting it ablaze. Arthur knew that he had to act fast if he was going to survive. He heard loud footsteps, alerting him that his opponent was very near.

With nerves of steel, he reloaded his pistol, emerged from his hiding place, and fired, taking out his human adversary in a flurry of shots. He didn't relish the violence, but he knew that it was necessary to protect himself.

With the immediate danger dealt with, Arthur barricaded the door to the console room and returned to his laptop. He continued to run his override script, his fingers flying over the keys as he worked to gain control of the ship's systems.

It was a perilous situation, but Arthur remained focused and determined. With a combination of cunning, skill, and sheer nerve, he was confident that he could emerge victorious.

* * *

Approximately two minutes later, a loud banging interrupted Arthur's work, making him jump. He quickly whipped around to see the door being forcefully struck by an unknown individual. The sound of someone almost attempting to smash the door open echoed through the room, and ten seconds of relentless pounding later, two sparks appeared on the door. It was evident to Arthur that someone was attempting to cut the door open.

Taking a brief moment to glance at his laptop, Arthur realized he was currently running a full-system shutdown, which was designed to brainwash the entire system and take control of it. However, he was now being interrupted, and this was bad news.

The banging on the door continued, and Arthur watched in horror as a hole was cut into the door, filling him with panic. He quickly realized that he did not want to resort to an all-out firefight, not only due to the ethical dilemma that presented itself but also because he could easily run out of ammo if he continued blasting away, and he was significantly outnumbered.

Despite the risks, Arthur had convinced himself that he should forge ahead. He had gotten so far already and would finish what he started.

Faced with the daunting task of dealing with the disturbance at the door, Arthur knew that hacking the robots was the solution, but the full-system shutdown left the robots inoperable. However, the override would take time, meaning that he needed to buy himself some time. The situation was becoming increasingly precarious, and the door was almost completely cut open, which meant that an all-out attack was imminent.

There was nothing he could do to speed up the override, so he began opening up all the supercomputers and running the same script he had used to create a makeshift bomb before, modifying it slightly because instead of a bomb, he needed a smokescreen. Arthur quickly gathered the necessary parts to make a giant makeshift smoke bomb, ensuring that the parts were not essential to the computers, so he could safely take them.

Once he had assembled the smoke bomb, he heard a loud creaking and banging noise and knew that the console room had been breached. A platoon of robots soon arrived, and Arthur activated the smoke bomb, which caused the excess heat energy that he had built up by stressing those machines out so much without proper cooling systems to release into the room. Smoke quickly filled the space, allowing Arthur to hide amidst the chaos of the fog.

As the smoke cleared, he heard a female voice say, "What the hell?" The platoon of robots had collapsed onto the ground due to the smoke infiltrating their systems, allowing Arthur to continue working on his laptop. He quickly executed the final commands and set up the developer console.

With a few simple lines of code, Arthur had cracked the system and was now the owner of the entire ship and its systems. The ship was machine-run, so he was the master of the machine. Finally, he typed in:

```
!set_access_permissions to [Current Device]
status=only
```

And:

```
!run control_hacker.script.
```

With this, Arthur had complete control. He just needed to type in a few more lines of code. He typed in:

```
!set_access_permissions to [Current Device]
status=only

SYSTEM RESPONSE: ONLY [Current device] NOW HAS
PERMISSION TO ACCESS THE SYSTEM

!run control_hacker.script

SYSTEM RESPONSE: RUNNING control_hacker.script...

SYSTEM: control_hacker.script_ successfully run.

set_commandsource=verbal

SYSTEM RESPONSE: SOURCE OF COMMANDS IS NOW SET TO
VERBAL.
```

Closing his laptop, he was suddenly conscious of something behind him. He felt the cold steel touch of a gun pressed against his head.

The woman he heard earlier was now behind him.

"Kiddo, you better explain yourself to the boss. Follow me."

Arthur muttered a curse under his breath.

CHAPTER V

Arthur's heart pounded as he was dragged through the dark, cavernous hallways of the ship, flanked by a fierce, gun-toting woman and a detachment of formidable robots. Although anxiety coursed through his veins, with sweat falling like a fountain from his forehead and his skin shivering profusely, he maintained a calm, collected demeanor on the surface, reminding himself of his command over the vessel. With a single verbal directive, he could summon the lethal firepower of the robots and decimate their captors. But he was determined to avoid an all-out fight, as he firmly believed that violence was never a viable solution.

They emerged from a long corridor to a set of double doors, which slid open easily, revealing a drab, gray office. Behind the large desk full of drawers was a bald man, who radiated authority. His posture was straight and his eyes fixed intently on the papers in front of him. His suit was impeccably tailored, and his cufflinks and watch gleamed in the light. He had an air of calm and composure about him that exuded authority and importance. His voice was deep and resonant, and when he spoke, it was with a measured confidence that made you listen and take notes. He exuded a powerful aura that filled the room, commanding attention and respect. It was clear that he was in charge, the captain of this ship, and that he knew what he was doing. His presence alone was enough to make you feel like you were in the presence of someone important, someone with the power to make things happen.

After a brief interlude of hushed conversation between the woman and an imposing man, the latter turned his attention to Arthur, his thick accent resonating across the chamber. "This young man has the temerity to infiltrate my ship and pillage it. Shameful!"

Arthur surveyed the room. He was in deep trouble, with a gun still pressed against the back of his head and facing the captain of his ship, while his personal belongings – including his trusty pistol, laptop, and pack – lay at the periphery under the watchful eye of the robots. However, the robots were his to command. All he needed to do was act. Do something. But somehow, nervousness finally started to seize him over. His whole body seemed to freeze in terror. The mild anxiety he managed to keep in check was now consuming him, and he could no longer maintain his cool demeanor to show that he wasn't afraid. He heard his teeth begin to clatter uncontrollably.

"I don't know where you're from, who you are, but you managed to almost hack my ship? That should not have happened, and you are going to pay for it. But before I kill you, I do want to know." the captain said, thoughtfully. He stacked his papers together and put them in a drawer.

"Either reveal your intentions or prepare to die a painful death once I eject you into space." the man threatened, his tone ominously low. For good measure, he produced a pistol from his pocket and pointed it at Arthur. "Ten seconds. Ten, nine-"

Arthur's mind raced furiously as he struggled to come up with an escape plan. "Seven, six, five-"

As he struggled to think of something, he knew he needed to act. He was in command of this whole ship. The captain had no authority over him, why was he terrified? The very robot pointing a gun to his head, at his command, would turn it to the pirates and send them back to their maker. Stop this anxiety and agitation, he told himself. What are you doing, trembling in fear for nothing?

"SHOOT THEM BOTH!" he yelled, his voice a hoarse shout.

The woman flinched in shock, and the man paused his counting. "What did you say?"

There was a small window of silence, and unease began to envelop Arthur again. Did his programming not work? Was there an override that he forgot to disable? The robots still pointed their weapons at him. His mind flew into a furious panic. What was he going to do?

Fortunately, Arthur's robotic programming kicked in, executing his verbal command. It seemed that the robots just had a delayed response. The androids turned their guns, and within moments, the woman crumpled to the ground, followed by the man who clutched his chest in agony. He writhed, yelped, and screamed as blood began to flow out of his wound.

Two human guards burst through the door, no doubt hearing the captain's shouts of pain, but the robots quickly dispatched them with laser-sharp precision.

With a sense of elation and relief, Arthur emerged from the office, his possessions - pistol, pack, and laptop - safely ensconced within his pack, which he held securely. "Scan the ship for any remaining life forms," he ordered the AI system.

The automated voice responded promptly. "No life signatures detected."

Arthur heaved a sigh of relief, as his control over the ship became absolute. Now, everything was automated, devoid of human intervention. He marveled at his audacity, having commandeered a derelict freighter and hacked into the ship's systems. More incredibly, he had emerged unscathed from a perilous, life-and-death situation, relying solely on his wits and ingenuity. His desperate ploy to confuse the humans and simultaneously issue commands to the robots had somehow paid off.

He strode purposefully toward the bridge, the robots trailing dutifully behind him. Despite the confusing labyrinth of wires and large control panel, his time on other ships had given him knowledge of what to do. Arthur brought up the navigation system and keyed in the *Nicholas's* coordinates. His hands flew over the controls, steering the ship back to the wreckage.

EPILOGUE

This is Kara Liss, reporting for BBC Intergalactic News.

In today's top story, a miraculous event has recently occurred. The crew of the expedition ship *Nicholas* has returned safely to Earth after several years of exploration. However, their journey was not without peril. While en route, the pirate heavy cruiser *Interstellar* attacked the *Nicholas* and her crew. Despite the destruction of the hyperspeed engines, Captain John Sents decided to jump to hyperspeed, causing an engine misfire that wrecked the ship.

Fortunately, crewmember Arthur Hood displayed remarkable bravery and ingenuity, sneaking off the ship in a light freighter to pursue the Interstellar. Hood managed to board the ship, hack its systems, and steer the cruiser back to the *Nicholas,* ultimately saving the crew and bringing them safely back to Earth.

As a result of his poor decision-making, Captain Sents was stripped of his status. Meanwhile, Hood was awarded the prestigious Victoria Cross for his heroic efforts in bringing the crew back to safety.

This incredible story serves as a testament to the bravery and dedication of our space explorers. We can only hope that their future missions will be met with less danger and more triumph.

The Robbery

* * *

STANLEY

This was going very badly.

So, all it took was 5 years for our entire friend group to fall apart. Ok, maybe that is expected. After leaving elementary school I lost touch with everyone, and I'm now a sophomore in high school. One night after going through my pile of homework (mostly math cus Mr. Drew hates us) I had a thought. Why not out of blue, reconnect with my old friends?

I'm amazed they even showed up, and nothing really happened. It's meant to be a karaoke night at this party place in Pasadena, but the machine only had like 30 songs and no one wanted to sing. Well, except George, who blew 5 songs before announcing his vocal cords needed a rest. Then Jeremiah left cus he needed to pack for a vacation in Barrow. First of all, why are you even going to Alaska, much less Barrow in the middle of winter, but I digress.

Then George put slugs in Tommy's shoes. Tommy was always George's prank victim and well, it seemed some things hadn't changed in 5 years.

After that, all 8 of us, George, Tommy, Julia, the Rhizzman sisters (Anne and Mary), Ted, and Robin. And I, of course, sat on the couch in awkward silence.

As the night wore, on we got 'the phone call' (insert dramatic music). And to make a long story short, everyone (except Anne and Mary for some reason) got a call from their parents, that their house had been burglarized, and when we all checked our jacket pockets, our keys were stolen. How *wonderful.* So a thief swiped our keys and burglarized our houses.

What a fantastic reunion. That's 100 dollars down the drain for some crappy party with a terrible karaoke machine, and getting robbed. I regretted trusting the review that this dump was the 'best karaoke place in LA'.

TOMMY

I mean, things could be worse. We got our keys stolen. Robbed, of very expensive stuff.

After Stanley's epic fail of a karaoke party a few days ago (seriously, how does a karaoke machine not have Wonderwall?), I'm now sitting on a bench in Arcadia Park. The sun is shining, and there's a gentle breeze blowing through the trees. The sounds of elementary school kids playing ninjas on the playground fill the air.

Then Stanley came walking towards me, dressed in a bright yellow hoodie and carrying his trusty black rucksack. He looks a bit down in the dumps, which is unusual for him. I wave and he gives me a weak smile.

Stanley normally (along with George, I guess) was just one of those dudes which were like, supercharged with energy, but I guess everybody's mood was down since the robbery. Oh yes, speaking of. Some anonymous thief somehow swiped our keys and went to our houses, and just took the most expensive things. My 500-dollar concert tickets, PC, and my mum's jewelry box got swiped clean from my house. Stanley had his entire tub of goldfish stolen, along with, of course, the expensive things like electronics and jewelry. Almost all of my friend's electronics got stolen. Robin and her family were one of the families who were very paranoid, and all her security cameras and alarms her parents spend way too much on were also stolen.

How's it going?" I ask, trying to sound casual. I'm feeling a bit nervous, to be honest. Ever since the robbery, things have been tense between us.

"Ah, well," he said. His tone was clearly sad and depressed, and his normally cheerful expression turned into a sour frown.

"Could be worse. Aside from my- g-goldfish, only expensive stuff was stolen. It's fine. I don't cry in my sleep! I totally don't. Anyways, why are we here, again? Yes, just text me to come over to this random bench in the park."

"I'm about to explain that," I said. "Once George comes."

"Oh, George is coming as well?"

"Yeah. Be careful though, his TV got snatched."

"Is he still addicted to TV?"

"Yup. God-knows how many hours he spends on Netflix binging every show there is."

"Speak of the devil," Stanley said.

George walked up to the bush. From what I remember, you can always tell his mood by his LA Dodgers baseball cap. If it's backward, he's happy or at least neutral. Forward is when he's serious, and if it's janked up like it is right now, to the side and not even worn properly. I think it has something to do with when he puts it on in the morning.

He sat down and pushed his cap over his face, hiding his very melancholic face.

We sat in a very awkward silence for like a solid 30 seconds before George suddenly looks up and said, "Why are we here?"

"I was about to explain that," I said. "So, basically, I called us here to discuss the whole, robbery situation. I have a suspicion, right, that Anne and Mary were the ones that took our keys!"

At this point, George fell off his chair in laughter (30 seconds ago this guy was the saddest man on earth for losing his TV). Stanley sniggered.

"What's so funny?" I asked as they both laughed.

"OK, I get that you're bummed you got robbed, and we all got robbed, but why are you pointing the fingers at the Rhizzman sisters?" George said, still chuckling. "We've been friends with Anne and Mary for what, 8 years?"

"10," Stanley said, counting his fingers.

"Exactly," George said. "And I'm busy with a mountain of homework, so it would be appreciated if I-"

"Stop. Stop. Hear me out, OK?" I said. "First of all, Anne and Mary's keys haven't been stolen. And secondly, they didn't get a phone call. Doesn't that seem suspicious?"

"How would we know that?" George shot back.

"Didn't you read the group chat?" I asked.

"No, why would I? It's been inactive for 5 years," George said, shrugging.

"Well, we've been talking and exchanging stories, and they were the only ones whose keys hadn't been stolen. So, I think it's kind of sus. And at the party, the Rhizzmans didn't get any phone calls. And also, how did a thief steal our keys anyway?"

"They might have snuck into the party room and swiped them," Stanley replied.

"That doesn't seem possible," George said.

"Exactly! So-"

"Wait-," Stanley said, cutting me off. "You're telling me you think someone, within friends we've known since elementary school, stole our keys and burglarized us. What a likely story."

"No," I said, "But it's suspicious, alright? That they didn't get their keys stolen and didn't get a phone call. "

"Alright. Fine. I'll send them a text and ask them, how 'bout that?" Stanley said, taking out his phone.

"Woah. Hold your horses. First of all, you're just blindly pointing fingers at the Rhizzmans. That is very rude. If I got accused I think I would smack you 'round the face and say that you're stupid. Second of all, what're you going to say to them? They didn't get their keys stolen, OK, but they still got robbed, right?" George cut in.

"Says the person who doesn't read the group chat," I said. "Yes, I think they got robbed, but isn't it weird-"

"There are many ways of entering a house without keys. Maybe the thief didn't have time to grab the Rhizzmans' keys. They could easily smash a window and break in," George said.

"Yeah, speaking of which, it probably isn't one thief. They stole TVs and heavy stuff. I think Robin got her solar panels grabbed. So it's gotta be at least 2 people. And also, Anne and Mary might know something about the robbery but they don't know, right?" Stanley said.

"Ok, how about we maybe just send a text to ask them to meet up and we can ask questions? Because I think they know something that we don't, about the robbery," I suggested.

"What's your evidence for that?" George questioned.

"Um-" the truth was, I simply found the fact their keys hadn't been stolen, and they didn't get a phone call suspicious and the rest was all just hunches.

"None," I said carefully, "But it wouldn't hurt to-"

"No. This is a bad idea," George said. "We're accusing Anne and Mary of total nonsense, and-"

"Well," Stanley cut in. "I sent a text already, so, yeah."

"What? No- uhh," George groaned. "Fine, let's ask them and bust your stupid theory about how it's suspicious that they didn't get their keys stolen. I'm telling you, it's a coincidence."

"No, it's not," I said. Suddenly, I became aware that I felt something slimy and wet in my shoe. I looked down. There doesn't seem to be anything wet on the ground. It hadn't rained in a week. And worst of all, it seemed that the mysterious thing inside my shoe was- *moving.*

"Guys, my shoe feels weird. It's like there's something slimy-"

"Oh yeah!" George said, all of a sudden, his voice very cheerful now. "I put slugs in your shoes. Bye!"

"You WHAT?" I roared, but George was already long gone, leaving Stanley and me on the bench. I took off my shoe and sure enough, there was a very disgusting, and slimy slug, worming around. I almost threw up in disgust as I shook it off, took a piece of tissue, and did my best to wipe it off. Stanley sniggered at the situation.

"It's not funny! First time I'd seen him in 5 years and he puts slugs in my shoe. A few minutes ago he was so sad, and now he's the happiest man alive and has the mood to put a slug in- I swear, someone needs to stop him from pranking me. Why me?"

"I guess some things haven't changed. You're still a prime target of George's practical jokes," he said, chuckling. "Cheer up, man. You wanna go get In-N-Out or something? I'm hungry."

"I could go for an In-N-Out burger," I said. "Ok, let's go then."

TED

Despite the fact, Julia, Robin, and the Rhizzmans all go to the same all-girls high school as me, I never really talked to them.

So I was surprised when I sat down for the after-school study group in the hall that the teachers host for 'students with potential' which is a contradiction of what it actually means, that we don't have enough 'potential' and need extra backing up on subjects, Julia sat next to me and opened her laptop.

"Hi," I said.

She waved.

"So, um," I thought of something to make conversation. "How're the grades?"

"Terrible. I aimed for an A+, I only got straight As."

I wonder what the teachers were thinking putting Julia, the one with straight As consistently in a study group for people like me who gets Cs and Ds.

"Um, ok. I got Cs and one B."

"No wonder you're here," she said.

Ok, same old Julia, the one who's brutally honest about every-thing, and I mean everything. She has no concept of when you need to lie about something. She once told a guy who looked like someone barfed color over his clothes to get new ones and almost got beat up.

"So um, how was the whole robbery thing?" I asked.

"Terrible as well. My $4000 telescope got stolen and it's almost comet season!"

Ahh yes. The nerd in the group, who's into stargazing for some reason.

"Ok-ay. Um-"

"Hello," came a voice out of nowhere, and Robin sat down at the table behind us.

"Hi, Robin," we said in unison.

"How's life?" I asked.

"Could be worse," she said. "So we girls are sitting together now?"

"I guess," I replied. "With the whole robbery thing."

"Yeah. My security cameras got stolen, my solar panels, my TV, and my iPad. The security is connected to my iPad, and without all those stuff anyone can just walk into my house! What am I going to-"

"Re-lax!" I said, cutting her off before she goes into a rant. "Stop being so paranoid! Your house has a *lock* for a reason!"

Robin's mouth opened as if to say something, but then clamped shut and reached into her rucksack to get her notes out. At this point, the teacher arrived. The hall, which in addition to ours was lively with conversation, was now a plain of silence.

I got out my notes and listened as Mrs. Jones booted up the projector and started droning about algebraic problems while we all took notes.

10 minutes later while Mrs. Jones was deep in an explanation about equation solving when Robin leaned over and whispered, "I have a theory, y'know,"

"What?" I whispered back.

"A theory. About the robbery,"

"Not now, Robin," I said, writing down an example equation.

"I think Anne and Mary, you know the Rhizzmans? They stole our keys."

I froze for a second before letting out a chuckle. "What?"

"I said, Anne and Mary-"

"Yes," I said, "I got that part. Are you crazy?"

68

"My mom knows a therapist," Julia said. "Perhaps this whole situation has caused a mental breakdown. That happens. You know, when you get robbed of everything expensive you own. She has fair prices."

"No, I'm not crazy!" Robin hissed. "I think that Anne and Mary stole our keys! They didn't get *their* keys stolen, so they must have stolen ours!"

"Yeah, right," I said, laughing.

"OK, they didn't get their keys stolen. That makes them super suspicious."

"Yeah, and? They got lucky. Fate smiled at them. Now can I please concentrate on negative number equations?"

"Y'know, Robin kind of has a point," Julia said.

" What are you talking about?" I asked, shaking my head.

"They didn't get their keys stolen, and did they even get robbed at all?"

"No, we all got robbed–"

Just at this moment, Anne came into the study hall. She was always late to this thing and always had an excuse. This time, it was that apparently, she had diarrhea in the bathroom.

As she walked down the aisle, she saw us together and slid a chair over to sit down. "Hi. So we're sitting together now? What're we talking about?"

There was a bumbling silence, as we all felt awkward discussing Anne. Except for Julia, of course.

Before any of us could stop here, she said, "Oh, we were talking about you."

"Me? What are you talking about?"

Robin's hand shot out to try to stop Julia, but before she did, she started talking. "Robin had an idea that you didn't get your keys stolen."

Anne shifted uncomfortably. "What are you on about, eh?"

"She said that you didn't get your keys stolen."

"I didn't get my keys stolen? Of course, I did!" Anne said.

"No, I saw you go into your house just fine. When I saw Tommy try to get into his house he had to break a window," Robin said.

"It was my parents' set of keys, OK? Honestly, what are you on about? Saying I didn't get my keys stolen."

"No, you didn't get your keys stolen. You were the only one who didn't complain in the group chat your keys were stolen."

Anne seemed to take a deep breath. "OK, fine, I didn't get my keys stolen. But I did get robbed."

"Why didn't your keys get stolen-"

"I don't know," Anne said. "Maybe the thief ran out of time!"

"Then why didn't your security go off? Because if the thief didn't have your keys, he would break a window or force himself in, which would trigger your motion sensor. I know your phone is connected to the security system. If it did go off, your phone would start ringing loudly. And also, you didn't get a phone call!"

"Yes I did," Anne said defensively. "I did get a phone call. Mary got one cus we were together."

"No, she didn't. When our parents called us about how our houses have been burglarized, you and Mary did not get any phone calls. Zip. Nada," Robin pressed on.

"I got a phone call," Anne said. "And I got robbed. Stop asking!" her face, for some reason, started to turn red.

"Ok, what things got taken? Cus we all got TVs and jewelry taken, what about-"

"Guys, stop this-" I held up my hand. They were now just accusing Anne of apparently being responsible. "I know we're all bummed we got robbed, but why are you blaming-"

"Shut up, Ted," Robin said. "Anyways, what did you get robbed of?"

"Um," Anne seemed very nervous, as she played with her fingers and shifted uncomfortably. "A jumper. My sweater got stolen. A bunch of jackets. Leggings."

"Wait a sec," Julia said. "My $4000 telescope got stolen and you have the nerve to tell me that only your sweater, jackets, and leggings got stolen. What?"

"No-"

"Girls?" Mrs. Jones' voice echoed through the study hall. "Would you like to say something to the class? You seem very absorbed in conversation."

Before Julia could blurt something out, I spoke up. "No, Mrs. Jones. Sorry." I dropped my head down and pretended to take more notes.

"I'm gotta get to the bottom of this mess," Julia said. "I have a cousin, Amelia, she knows everything about everyone and everything. She'll get to the bottom of this."

"No, what are you guys talking about? Why are you-" Anne said, her tone seeming desperate for some reason before her mouth clamped shut as she got a deathly stare from Mrs. Jones.

MARY

I was lounging on my bean bag, playing my Nintendo when Anne's call interrupted my game.

I pressed pause and picked up my phone."I thought you were still in school in the study group thing," I said, puzzled.

"I finished my study hall early," she replied, her voice tense. "Listen, they're onto us."

"What are you talking about?" I asked.

"You know the thing?" she said.

"Oh, that," I said, understanding dawning on me.

"Shhh!" Anne hushed me. "Be quiet!"

"They can't track our calls, Anne," I assured her. "Relax."

"But they're suspicious," she continued. "Today at the study group, Julia and Robin—not so much Ted—were talking about how they think we stole their keys."

"What? How did they figure that out?"

"I don't know. Robin said that we didn't get our keys stolen and that we took theirs instead."

I took a deep breath, trying to stay calm. This was bad. How did Robin shoot into the dark and hit a target? "Okay, we need to come up with a good excuse. What did you tell them?"

"I said our sweater and leggings got stolen," Anne blurted out.

"What? Anne, why would you say that?" I exclaimed, my voice rising in panic. "They had expensive stuff stolen, and you tell them about clothes from the dollar store?"

"Not the dollar store, they were from Abercrombie," she protested weakly.

"Still not the best excuse," I said, trying to keep my voice level. "They're definitely onto us now."

"I know, I messed up," Anne said, sounding defeated.

"It's okay," I reassured her. "We just need to protect Jeremiah. Let's come up with a better plan and stick to it. We got this."

GEORGE

So for the second time this week, I'm sitting on a bench in a park, next to the iTennis center at the north end of Arcadia Park. Tommy and Stanley were next to me.

"So. Why are we here again?" I asked.

Tommy sighed. "This is the what, 5th time I have to explain this to you. We're meeting the rest of the gang to discuss this whole situation. And also-"

"Yes, we're going to ask Anne and Mary whether they stole our keys, but I think that theory needs more evidence. We've been friends for what, 10 years? Why would they do such a thing?" Stanley cut in.

"I agree. This is ridiculous," I said. "You're just bummed out you can't go to the Iron Maiden concert. Who even listens to heavy metal?

"Shut up. You listen to-"

"Hello," came a voice out of nowhere, interrupting us. Ted, Robin, and Julia had arrived, along with a new girl I didn't know. She wore a full black getup, including a leather jacket and boots, and her raven-black hair was styled in a messy bun.

"Hi," Stanley said. We scooted over to allow them room, which isn't much considering the bench was meant for only 3 people. We crowded together on the bench.

"Why are we here?" Julia said immediately as she tried to make herself comfortable on the very overcrowded bench. In the distance, the sounds of tennis players were heard in the distance of the *pop* of ball hits.

"This is the third time I've had to explain," Tommy said. "We're here, waiting for Anne and Mary, because I want to ask them some questions, OK? And you decided to tag along."

"Oh, yes, now I remember," Julia said.

"Who's that girl in the black getup?" I asked.

"Oh," Julia said. "That's my cousin, Amelia, and she knows everything about everyone and everything around the neighborhood."

"Is she nosy or just well-connected?" I asked.

"I like to think of myself as well-connected," Amelia said, smiling. "Julia called me because apparently, your friend Tommy had a theory that you guys thought that the Rhizzmans stole your keys?"

"I was thinking the same thing!" Robin said.

"Which is completely ridiculous, why would they do that?" I asked, shaking my head.

"Of course, you would, Robin," I said. "You'd think a spider crawled away with your security cameras if it got too close to your house. Stop being so paranoid."

"I have every right to be suspicious of the Rhizzmans," she shot back. "All of our security never got triggered because the thief had our keys so, they bypassed all the security features. Anne told us that she did get robbed, but if the thief didn't have your keys, he would break a window or force himself in, which would trigger your motion sensor. I know her phone is connected to the security system. If it did go off, her phone would start ringing loudly. And also, she didn't get a phone call!"

"She told Anne that," Ted added.

"Well, the Rhizzmans did get robbed so I don't see what all the fuss is. They've been our friends for 10 years, everything is a coincidence, why are we shooting into the dark?" I asked.

"Actually," Amelia spoke up. "Your friends' theory holds up pretty well. From the information Julia gave me, the Rhizzman sisters didn't get phoned about getting burglarized or getting their keys stolen, they confessed to the latter. Secondly, her lie about 'getting robbed' is ridiculous. Who goes into a house and steals clothes?"

"Clothes?" Stanley asked.

"Yeah. She said the robbers took a sweater, jackets, and leggings," Amelia replied.

"That seems a bit stupid, but it's just a coincidence, OK?" I said.

"How can you think that? What, your plasma TV got swiped and all the Rhizzmans got robbed of are clothes?" Robin said.

"Oh wow, George," Amelia said. "You really are blind."

"What are you talking about?!" I said, standing up before Tommy placed an enormous arm in the way and pushed me back onto my seat.

"I agree with Robin and Tommy. That's because Jeremiah and the Rhizzmans did it."

The group fell silent, the only sounds coming from the distant pop of tennis balls and the rustling of leaves in the wind. Then, a collective, "What?"

"Jeremiah robbed you. He and his brother," Amelia said.

"What- he's on vacation in Alaska!" I exclaimed. "We're supposed to believe that he flew all the way from Alaska, back to LA, here, and robbed us. Julia, your cousin's a crackpot. She believes in a stupid theory Tommy and Robin cooked up and that Jeremiah, our long-time friend, and his brother robbed us."

"Let me explain. I've been investigating, snooping around, and talking to people, and I found out that Jeremiah and his brother are living in a run-down RV near Mayflower Avenue. I don't know why they're living in an RV, that I have no idea of. But I do know they don't have any money for anything, and they're desperate. His brother's hanging out with the wrong crowd and has been threatening him until he agreed to come to your party, steal your keys, and burglarized your houses for money. His brother drove the van, loaded up all your stuff, and left." Amelia said. "And the Rhizzman sisters? You guys stopped talking to each other until recently, but the 3 of them are still very close friends even after elementary school. When Jeremiah told them about the situation, they kept quiet about it to protect them. And since they're friends, he didn't burglarize their house at all."

"Everyone was silent for a moment, stunned as we all contemplated Amelia's words.

"What's your proof?" I asked. "And you're just making up Jeremiah's RV thing!"

"Stop denying it!" Robin said. "You know what she said is true! You live on Shrode Street next to Mayflower Avenue, your Dad literally drives you down that road to school, and you see it every day on your way to school. We should tell the police this."

"Fine. What Amelia said holds up. I saw that RV," I said, putting my hands up in defeat. "So what do we do now?"

"Well," Stanley said. "Maybe instead of *pointing fingers* at our *friends* behind their backs, we just wait for Anne and Mary to come, because I did invite them, and then we can ask them?"

We waited for a bit before Stanley got tired of waiting and went to the Rhizzmans' house, which was only a couple of houses away, to get them.

He came back 10 minutes later with Anne and Mary in tow. When they saw us, their eyebrows raised in confusion.

"What's going on? Stanley just walked up to our place and told us to come here outside the iTennis place, and now you guys are here," Mary said.

"Do you want to explain, or should I explain?" Tommy said.

"What are you guys talking about?" Anne asked.

"Well. Amelia, here, Julia's cousin, me, and Robin all had a theory, and we want to confirm it. We know you didn't get a phone call or get your keys stolen. You weren't even robbed. We know Jeremiah and his brother did it, and that you kept quiet. What we want to know, is why?"

The Rhizzmans jumped, and I mean literally, jumped in surprise, stuttering over their words.

"What are you talking about, wh-what-"

"I don't think lying in their faces is a good option, Anne," Mary said before Anne could start dumping her bucket of lies.

"Th-then-"

"There's no point lying. Yes, Jeremiah did it, but hear us out. His family, for some reason, has shattered and for some shape or reason, he didn't tell me, they've been kicked out of the house and now live in an RV. Their parents and relatives have been fighting and you do not want to know the details. Don't ask me more. They don't have money for anything, the RV doesn't have anything in it at all, and they're starving and desperate. So his brother, once he heard Jeremiah's meeting up with some old friends, told him to steal their keys and rob their houses. He disagreed, of course, but his brother threatened him or something. So he did it and robbed your stuff. We kept quiet to protect him, because with the whole situation we're in, he's going straight to prison, and it wasn't his fault it was his brother's, and- it's just a can of worms we didn't want to let loose really, so we kept quiet to protect him."

Another stunned silence. I hate a stunned silence, so I broke it.

"OK, so Jeremiah, robbed our stuff. Our friend since elementary school has robbed us."

"He really didn't want to, but he needed to do it, OK? He had no money. Please don't call the police on him..." Anne said.

"Where's our stuff, then? Has it-" Tommy began.

"It's been sold. Long gone," Mary replied.

We all swore under our breaths. "Sold? How much money did he need? If he asked us, we'd probably give him some money but-" Robin said.

"His brother told him to rob the expensive stuff. I told you, he's the mastermind. Jeremiah's just a pawn in his game," Mary said. "Please don't call the cops. I know it's-"

"I'm telling the police," Julia said firmly. "This is expensive stuff, you don't realize the gravity of this whole situation. Collectively, all of the things that have been burglarized probably add up to at least $10,000, maybe even more. The police already have an investigation going on, they'll find out eventually. How dare you keep quiet about this. You don't think this is significant just because you didn't get robbed. We all did, and all of our treasured possessions got swiped because you kept quiet about it. If you'd told us before the party, nothing would've happened. I'm going to phone the cops, and they're going to arrest Jeremiah. He's my friend, but he was an accomplice to this. I know his brother is to blame, but he could've just snuck out when he isn't looking to his friends, or to us and we would've helped. But he didn't, he went along with it. So I'm telling the cops, try to stop me."

She got up and left. Anne and Mary called after her in desperation, but it was no use. She continued forward, turning right towards the direction of the police station.

"So, anyone wanna go for an In-N-Out or Starbucks or something?" I asked.

Everyone stared at me.

"What? Julia's gone to tell the cops, all we have to do is wait now, and a fresh burger always lightens me up given this current situation," I said.

Stanley shrugged. "I guess. I could go for a Starbucks."